Death Walked In

A Play

Bettine Manktelow

A SAMUEL FRENCH ACTING EDITION

FOUNDED 1830

SAMUELFRENCH-LONDON.CO.UK
SAMUELFRENCH.COM

DEATH WALKED IN

First produced by the Acorn Players at The Granville
Theatre, Ramsgate, on 13th April, 1977, with the follow-
ing cast:

Angela Webster	Patricia Bryan
George Carter	David Collings
Joan Mountstevens	Bettine Manktelow
Celia Randolph	Sylvia Mason
Cdr. Roy Boothby	Laurie Bacon
Eva Mountstevens	Ruth Wilson
Rex Randolph	John Sparkes

Directed by Peter Nicolson

The action passes in the bar-lounge of a small country
hotel in Sussex

ACT I Scene 1 A September morning
       Scene 2 Evening, after dinner, two days later

ACT II Scene 1 One week later. Midday
       Scene 2 Early next morning

Time—the present

CHARACTERS

Angela Webster, waitress and general help, aged 18
George Carter, the gardener, aged 65+
Joan Mountstevens, aged 31
Celia Randolph, the hotel proprietress, aged 40+
Eva Mountstevens, aged 20+
Commander Roy Boothby, RN Retd, aged 60
Rex Randolph, aged 31

AUTHOR'S NOTE

The blonde wig is very important to the plot. If the actress is already blonde a red wig could be used instead, as long as it is sufficiently different from the hair of the other actresses for George to make a mistake over it.

It is suggested that "Love Walked In" is used as a theme tune, to be played as the Curtain rises on each scene.

B.M.

ACT I

SCENE 1

The bar/lounge of a small country hotel in Sussex

It is antique and quaint, having been converted from a Tudor manor house. The room is furnished with tables and chairs, a bar with bar stools, armchair and coffee table, and a record player. French windows lead on to a garden.

The archway entrance at the rear of the room leads on the right to the kitchen and the front door, and on the left to the bedrooms. There is a separate entrance to the bar (see ground plan on page 56). It is all very bright and neat but with a faintly neglected look to the place.

When the CURTAIN *rises Angela Webster is laying a table for breakfast. Angela, a sweet, unpretentious country girl, pretty but not very bright, is humming to herself. George Carter, a garrulous old man, inclined to be gloomy, weather-beaten with a marked Sussex accent, appears at the open french windows. Angela does not at first see him*

George I don't know what you've got to be so 'appy about.

Angela Oh, you made me jump! Creeping up like that.

George I wasn't creepin'. You was day-dreamin'.

Angela No I wasn't. What do you want anyway? You know you mustn't come in here with dirty boots.

George I'm not comin' in.

Angela The missus gets cross if you bring dirt in on her carpets. Besides, we've got some guests, two ladies booked in last night. They'll be comin' down to breakfast in a moment and they won't want your face peerin' at them while they eat.

George Missus about, is she?

Angela Not yet, but she won't be long. Why?

George I want to see 'er, that's why. Two ladies, is it?

Angela Yes, from London.

George Get lost, did they?

Angela What do you mean?

George Nobody comes 'ere by design, not these days.

Angela Some do.

George Not like the old days. Fair bustlin' with trade it was then.

Angela It'll pick up.

George That's what you think. If she took my advice, the missus, she'd sell up.

Angela Who'd buy it?

George She'd find somebody. Them Yanks that was here last week. They was taken with the place. Real cute they said it was. They ain't got nothing like this in Yankeeland.

Angela It's all right for a holiday, not to live in. I do wish you wouldn't distract me. I forget what I'm about—I've forgotten the marmalade.

She moves towards the archway

George 'Ere, wait a minute.

Angela What do you want?

George If you see the missus tell 'er we've got to get those plums in today. They're fair swarmin' with wasps, and if we don't pick 'em soon there won't be none left.

Angela What do you expect her to do about it? That's your job.

George So it may be, but I can't get up ladders at my age and with my arthritis, she knows that. I want her to get young Rex to come and help me.

Angela You'll be lucky! He was out on the tiles again last night. He's not even back as far as I know.

George If he won't help then they can stay there. I ain't clambering up that ladder at my age, not for nobody.

Angela All right, I'll tell her.

She turns to go as Joan appears in the archway

Joan Mountstevens is a rather plain, spinsterish schoolmarm; determined with a strong personality but with hidden depths of fire and passion. She has always repressed her true personality and her tension and somewhat neurotic preoccupation with the past are a result of this. On the surface she is cool, calm and matter of fact

Angela Oh, good morning, miss.

Joan Good morning. (*She looks across to the tables hesitantly*)

Angela Over by the window, miss, the table that's laid . . .

Angela dashes into the kitchen through the archway

Joan Thank you. (*She goes over to the table and stops when she sees George*) Oh, good morning.

George 'Morning. (*He stands watching Joan curiously as she sits at the centre table, facing front. There is a pause while George takes stock of her*) You arrived last night did you?

Joan Yes, that's right.

George Saw you driving through the village. I wondered if you was coming up 'ere.

Joan (*surprised*) You saw us, and you remember, well!

George (*pleased*) 'Course I do! There's not many strangers in the village these days. Nice little red car it was, foreign make, you and a blonde girl sitting in the front, I see you all right.

Joan (*she looks at George with sudden interest*) I've been here before, you know. I don't suppose you remember that?

George (*reflectively*) Now, let me see, 'ow long ago? I've lived 'ere all my life so I ought to remember.

Joan About ten years ago. I stayed here then.

George That was in the old man's days, good days they was. (*He looks at Joan keenly*) No, miss, can't say as 'ow I do remember you, but then in those days business was brisk, as they say, new people in and out all the time, fallin' over one another, they were.

Joan You were here then?

George Oh yes, miss, I've been here most of my life, except for the war. Used to be the odd-job man until me screws started playin' me up like, then I just got stuck with the gardenin'. That's enough for me, and too much sometimes. The old man and me, we used to 'ave a fair old time in the old days, drinkin' partners we were, and *he* could certainly knock 'em back, so could I in those days. A character he was and no mistake. (*He takes off his hat and scratches his head, chuckling to himself*)

Joan Yes, he was. I remember him well.

Angela returns with the marmalade

Angela (*breathlessly*) Sorry, miss, I forgot the marmalade.

Joan That's all right. I'm in no hurry.

Angela What are you doing standing there, George Carter? I'll tell the missus what you said.

George Just goin', just goin'. No harm done. God preserve me from naggin' women.

George goes, muttering to himself

Angela Nosey old thing! Now, miss, what would you like, tea or coffee?

Joan Tea, please, and some toast. Nothing cooked.

Angela Oh, that's nice and easy. What about the other lady?

Joan My sister? Oh, I doubt whether she'll be able to face a cooked breakfast, but I suppose you'd better ask her yourself. She won't be long.

Angela Yes, miss, all right. I mean madam. The missus keeps telling me I must say madam, but I forget.

Joan Have you been here long?

Angela No. Just this summer. Before that I was in the fields, but I didn't like it. Ruined my 'ands.

Joan Yes it would.

Angela turns to go

Are we the only guests?

Angela (*turning round*) At the moment you are. Except for the Commander, of course, and he doesn't count because he's a resident.

Joan Ah yes, the Commander, I met him last night. A charming man, I thought.

Angela Yes, he's ever so nice, isn't he? Not a bit stuck-up. He's an old friend of the missus. He's lived here for about a year, I think. (*She once more turns to go*)

Joan (*abruptly*) I was here before you know.

Angela (*turning back; a little impatiently*) Oh? When?

Joan About ten years ago. Before your time.

Angela Has it changed much?

Joan The place itself, no, not a bit. I'm pleased about that. I was afraid it might have changed.

Angela That must have been when the old man was alive, Mr Randolph.

Joan Yes, that's right. He ran it with the help of his son, Rex.

Angela Oh, Rex is still here, of course. You didn't know the missus then? I mean Mrs Randolph—no, you wouldn't have done. He only married her a few months before his death. She was the receptionist, you know, that's all.

Joan Oh, yes . . .

Angela (*beginning to enjoy a gossip*) Took everyone by surprise it did, in the village, when old Mr Randolph up and married his receptionist. Years older than her he was, I mean to say, she's not much older than her own step-son. Funny, really, isn't it?

Joan It does happen. It's not all that extraordinary . . .

Celia appears in the bar entrance

Celia Randolph is a sophisticated, self-possessed woman with an imperious manner. Superficially she appears very hard, but this conceals emotions which are just under control. She is worried and abstracted most of the time

Angela (*confidentially*) Still, there's been some funny talk . . .

Joan (*seeing Celia over Angela's shoulder*) Yes, dear, that will be all, just tea and toast.

Angela Eh? (*She turns round and seeing Celia moves up to the archway*) Oh, good morning, Mrs Randolph. Old George wants a word with you, about picking the plums.

Celia Yes, all right. I'd appreciate my coffee first if you don't mind.

Angela Right away, Mrs Randolph.

Angela exits through the archway

Celia (*coming down-stage to Joan*) Good morning, Miss Mountstevens, did you sleep well?

Joan Yes, thank you, like a top.

Celia That's our good Sussex air. Everybody says the same. I do hope Angela hasn't been boring you with her chatter. She's rather a talkative girl. It's her one fault.

Joan No, she wasn't a bit boring. (*She pauses*) I was telling her that I'd been here before. It seemed to interest her.

Celia Yes, I suppose it would. Rex isn't back yet. I shall tell him as soon as I see him.

Joan He probably won't remember me.

Celia I don't know. He has a pretty good memory for customers, particularly of the feminine gender.

Joan It was a long time ago. I've changed.

Celia He hasn't. He's like Peter Pan, he never will grow up. What about the hotel? Do you notice any difference here?

Joan Not really. I was quite pleased when I drove through the gateway yesterday and saw how little it had changed. It's such a beautiful place, the ivy and the grey stone, and the latticed windows. I think I fell in love with it all over again. I've often been back here in my dreams.

Celia I see it captured your imagination. It does that to some people.

Joan Yes, that's right. There's a kind of magic quality about it, as if it isn't quite real.

Celia It's real enough, so are the bills.

Joan You sound rather despondent.

Celia A little perhaps. You can't have failed to notice that business isn't exactly thriving.

Joan I was a bit surprised to find that no-one else is staying here, except for the Commander. Has it been like this long?

Celia Not really. But this year has been particularly bad. They built a motorway that by-passed the village, that was the first thing. It cut us off. It's so hard to find us now that people get tired of looking, at least that's what I think happened. Now I just feel as if there's a jinx on the place.

Joan No, it can't be as bad as that. You'll see, things will get better. At least you have Rex to help you.

Celia (*looking thoughtfully at Joan*) Mm, yes, I have Rex.

Angela enters with tea and toast on a tray

Angela Here you are, madam, and your sister's just coming down the stairs as well.

Joan Thank you, dear.

Angela I've made your coffee, Mrs Randolph. (*She begins to unload the tray on the table at which Joan is sitting*)

Celia Oh, thank you. I'll see you later Miss Mountstevens.

Celia exits through the archway

Joan Yes, I look forward to it.

Angela (*looking over her shoulder to make sure Celia has gone*) I hope she wasn't cross with me, talking to you. She doesn't like us being too friendly with the guests.

Joan She didn't say anything.

Angela That's a relief. I wouldn't like to lose my job. I mean the pay's not all that good, but it's better'n working on the land.

Joan Don't worry about it. Anyway, I was at fault for encouraging you.

Angela It's hard to resist a bit of gossip when you can see somebody's interested, isn't it? (*She giggles*) The country's a terrible place for gossip. Such stories goes round the village, you'd never believe.

Joan Try me.

Angela (*tempted*) Well . . . (*She looks over her shoulder and bends forward*)

Eva appears in the doorway. Angela straightens up

Eva Mountstevens is young, pretty, selfish and amoral. Unlike her sister she appears to be what she is, only more so. She is intent upon burning up her youth in the pursuit of pleasure

Joan Never mind. Some other time.

Angela Yes, all right. Morning, miss.

Eva Morning. (*She slouches into the room and slumps down in the chair opposite Joan, scowling at her*)

Joan (*sweetly*) Good morning, dear, did you sleep well?

Eva Unfortunately, too well. I feel horrible. I only got up now because I'm thirsty. You might have arranged for me to have a cup of tea in bed.

Joan I didn't think about it, sorry.

Angela Would you like bacon and egg, miss?

Eva Ugh!

Joan I think that means no, Angela.

Angela Coffee or tea?

Joan There's enough tea here for both of us, dear, don't bother.

Angela All right then. Just ring that little bell if you want me.

Angela exits through the archway

Joan (*pouring out the tea*) I take it you have a hangover.

Eva Don't look so pleased about it.

Joan (*smugly*) I told you not to drink so much last night.

Eva What else is there to do in this God-forsaken hole? *You* were all right chatting up that ancient commander, but he wasn't my type. What was I supposed to do?

Joan Precisely what you did, I suppose, get drunk. I should be grateful you didn't make a scene.

Eva I don't make scenes all the time. I was too bored even to do that. I kept hoping lover boy would come in and liven things up a bit.

Joan (*irritably*) I wish you wouldn't refer to him like that. He was just a friend, just somebody I used to know, nothing special.

Eva Oh yeah?

Joan Yes, believe it or believe it not.

Eva Anyway, once you've looked him over I hope we'll be able to pass on. We don't have to stay here the whole week, do we? It's strictly dullsville. No fun, no men! It's not my idea of a holiday place at all. We're not far from Brighton, we could spend a few nights there.

Joan (*firmly*) Listen, Eva. We came on this holiday so that you could recuperate from—various things. You promised me it would be a quiet holiday and since I was paying I could choose the route.

Eva I was feeling so low at the time I would have promised anything, but hell, that was two weeks ago now.

Joan The bargain still stands as far as I'm concerned.

Eva But why come here? You couldn't have chosen a bigger dump.

Joan I like it. Besides we were so close I couldn't resist just having a look at it again to see if it had changed.

Eva Well, you've had a look and it hasn't changed, so let's go.

Joan We'll see.

Eva Otherwise I'll go without you.

Joan And without any money?

Eva To hell with money. I'll hitchhike, and shack up with the first available guy I meet. How would that suit you?

Joan (*wearily*) I really believe you would. You'll never learn, will you? (*She pushes her plate away impatiently, knocking over the bell*)

Eva I'd do anything to get away from here. I woke up feeling so depressed. I warn you if we spend another night here I shall do something desperate, like seduce the Commander—God help him!

Joan (*with an effort, controlling her temper*) Sometimes, Eva, I have the most uncharitable thoughts about you.

Eva That does worry me!

Angela enters

Angela I thought I heard the bell.

Joan No, but it doesn't matter, you can clear. I seem to have lost my appetite. (*She rises, glares at Eva and crosses the room to the armchair, picking up a magazine and glancing through it to keep her temper from showing*)

Eva (*snatching her cup from the table*) *I* haven't finished.

Angela (*hesitantly*) I'm sorry—I'll come back . . .

Eva It's all right! (*She finishes her tea and hands Angela the cup, then she rises and stands poised between the window and the table, while Angela begins to clear*)

Eva (*lighting a cigarette*) Tell me, since you're a native of these parts, what do people do around here for kicks?

Angela (*clearing the table and stacking things on her tray*) Kicks?

Joan (*drily*) Perhaps they have a donkey in the stable.

Angela No, miss, we 'aven't. There's a riding stable in the village though, if you're interested.

Eva (*sighing impatiently*) I mean what do people do to amuse themselves?

Angela Oh, go to the pub, play darts, things like that. There's a disco every Friday in the village hall, and the missus gets a good crowd up here on a Saturday night—Young Conservatives.

Eva Oh God! My table tennis just isn't up to it!

Angela (*puzzled*) There's a snooker table in the other bar, but we 'aven't got anywhere to play table tennis, I'm afraid.

Joan Don't take any notice of her, Angela. She's having you on.

Angela (*rather hurt*) Oh, I see. Sorry, I'm sure.

Eva How do people live here? It's beyond me.

Angela (*defensively*) We 'ave to make our own amusement in the country.

Eva (*amused*) Don't tell me there's something I've missed! (*looking out of the window idly*) Ah, I spy an approaching car! Could it be a visitor! Where are my binoculars?

Angela (*scornfully*) That's not a visitor! That's Rex, back from Brighton. *He* always seems to find plenty to occupy him, I must say.

Eva I like the car. Just my style, long sleek lines . . . I'm curious to see the occupant.

Joan (*trying to appear casual, walks over to the window*) It's a sports car. He always liked fast cars.

Eva (*with a disparaging look at Joan*) And slow women!

Angela He likes variety, does Rex. Tell you what though, his cars last longer than his women do. He gets very attached to his cars.

Eva (*softly*) He's beginning to interest me. (*She steals a look at Joan*)

Joan is tight-lipped and does not react to this remark. Angela has cleared and makes a movement towards the door with her loaded tray

Angela (*to Joan*) Shall I tell him you're here?

Joan (*nervously*) I don't know.

Eva Why not keep it as a surprise?

Joan He might not want to meet people just now if he's been up all night. He'll be tired.

Angela Not 'im. He's like his old man, constitution like an ox. I'll tell 'im. He's bound to come through the kitchen looking for something to eat. He's always ravenous when he's been up all night.

She exits through the archway

Eva (*rising*) I think I'll go and tidy up.

Joan You look perfectly all right now.

Eva I think I could look better. (*with a wicked grin*) You want me to make a good impression on your old flame, don't you?

She moves towards the archway but before she reaches it the Commander enters with two newspapers under his arm. She gives him a mock salute

Eva Good morning, Commander.

Commander Good morning, you're full of the joys of spring!

Eva I'm just beginning to realize this holiday could be fun.

She exits through the archway L. with a last look at Joan

Commander I'm surprised she's so bright and breezy this morning after last night.

He comes into the room. Commander Roy Boothby is an elderly man with a military bearing. He is cultured, affable and easy-going, polite and un-flappable. His keen intelligence is somewhat hidden by his courteous manner

Joan I must apologize for my sister. I'm afraid she's rather—uninhibited in her behaviour.

Commander Oh, it's refreshing. I don't mind a bit.

Joan (*she is nervous and making conversation*) Have you had your break-fast? Shall I call Angela?

Commander No. I never eat breakfast, thanks. I've just been down to the village for the papers. It saves the boy a long drag up here, and it does me good.

Joan I must say we did enjoy the conversation last night. It was very interesting.

Commander I thought afterwards I'd rather talked too much. Loquacity is the curse of old age! (*He sits comfortably in the armchair and opens his paper*)

Joan Oh, not in your case. You've had such an interesting life people love to hear you talk about it. You don't know how I envy you travelling all over the world.

Commander (*modestly*) Yes, I think I've been around more than most. But it was all thanks to my job.

Joan Intelligence work must be fascinating, especially in wartime.

Commander Yes and no. It has its darker side.

Joan I suppose so. (*Her attention wanders to the archway, waiting for someone to appear; with an effort she turns back to the Commander*) Why don't you write a book about it?

Commander It's been done to death. Anyway I couldn't tell the truth.

Joan Why not?

Commander (*enigmatically*) Secrets are still secrets, even thirty years after.

Joan Oh. (*Nervously, still with one eye on the archway*) It must be a strange life living permanently in an hotel.

Commander I like it. I've always lived in hotels or else in some officers' mess somewhere. I'm a pariah. I had a home briefly in Hong Kong when I was married, but it didn't last long.

Joan What, the home or the marriage?

Commander Neither.

Joan I'm sorry.

Commander It's too long ago to worry me now.

Joan (*with genuine interest*) What made you decide to settle down here, in this hotel, miles from anywhere?

Commander It's a beautiful place, isn't it? I love antiquity. I like the area. Besides I've known Celia for years. I like to be around in case she needs a shoulder to cry on.

Joan I see. (*She sits down-stage and then nervously rises again at once. She tries again to make conversation*)

The Commander looks at her shrewdly

Commander Habits of a lifetime are hard to break.

Joan (*making conversation and still straining to hear something off-stage*) Don't you ever have any breakfast?

Commander A glass of tonic water with honey and wine vinegar, that's my breakfast.

Joan Oh? (*She shudders*) It sounds awful! (*She sits down-stage* R.)

Commander It keeps me fit.

Rex Randolph enters and stands in the archway

Rex Randolph is a good-looking, thirtyish man with great charm. He knows he has sex-appeal and uses it to the best of his advantage. He is also blessed with an attractive personality and great confidence. On the darker side of his character he is weak and has no sense of direction. He drifts in whichever direction the current pleasure takes him. He has no real depth

Joan rises nervously. He goes over to her

Rex Angela tells me we're old friends.

Joan (*nervously*) I stayed here once—a long time ago.

Rex Of course, I remember, Joan Mountstevens, that was the name, wasn't it?

Joan (*with relief*) Yes, that's right.

They shake hands

Rex Well after all these years! What a surprise! What do you think of that Roy? This good lady knew me in the good old days when the hotel was really thriving and I was a mere hirsute youth.

Joan (*laughing*) You weren't at all hirsute.

Commander Yes, she was telling me about it last evening. The hotel must have been quite different then—when the old man was alive.

Rex I'll say it was . . .
Joan Not so very different . . . } (*Together. Then they stop and laugh*)

Rex I think it was different. Surely, it was much more fun . . .

Joan Yes, that I suppose. But the place itself. It's just as beautiful as ever.

Rex One gets used to that. It's the business we miss.

Joan Of course.

Rex We were always full up in those days. Now that the motorway has come and by-passed the village we're quite forgotten. You need a compass to find the place.

Joan But some people like a quiet holiday.

Rex Unfortunately, not enough. However, that's our problem, not yours. Tell me about when you were here before, refresh my memory.

Joan (*pleased*) I was staying here with another teacher. We'd just finished our training at college and were going out into the wide world. There was another young man who was always here, a friend of yours. We used to go out in a foursome a lot. You had an old banger, a Ford of some kind. It got stuck in bottom gear in Littlehampton once, and we had to drive all the way back at about ten miles an hour.

Rex Yes, I remember—good lord! That was old Barry Roberts—he's married now, you know, got three kids, poor chap.

Joan My friend was very taken with him. She's married too now. She didn't teach for more than a year, such a waste of her training.

Rex Oh yes, quite! And what about you? You married?

Joan No. (*With Pride*) I'm Deputy Head of a secondary modern school in Richmond, actually.

Rex (*impressed*) Well!

Joan And you?

Rex What?

Joan You haven't married?

Rex Good lord no! I've never seen the necessity—I mean, I've just never met the right girl.

Joan I see. (*She moves away from him thoughtfully*)

The Commander, meanwhile, though reading his paper, is nonetheless listening to the conversation. Sometimes, he looks over the top of the paper at the others, but only when they are not looking his way

Joan There are so many things I remember about that year. I was thinking about them last night in bed. We used to dance in here to some old seventy-eights that belonged to your father. Do you remember?

Rex Of course, we've still got them in the attic. I'll look them out while you're here.

Joan Dick Haymes was his favourite. He didn't mind how often we played his records.

Rex Couldn't stand them myself.

Joan Sweetly sick nostalgia. I know now why he liked them, they reminded him of his youth. I can understand that now.

Rex What else did we do? You've got a much better memory than I.

Joan Swimming, tennis, all the usual things. We went out for a picnic once, and it rained. Coming back across the field, over there . . . (*She points through the window*) We found a dead fox. It must have been caught in a combine harvester. There was blood across its stomach. I've never forgotten it, finding him out there among the stubble, so stiff and sad and lonely, the blood almost black on his red fur. There was a beauty in it.

Rex You *have* got a good memory.

Joan Only for certain things.

Rex They were carefree days though, before the old man died. It's all different now.

Joan You haven't changed.

Rex Oh, but I have. I'm quite thin on top. And I can't live it up like I used to.

Joan (*fondly*) I haven't noticed.

Rex No, really, take last night. I could normally take a sleepless night in my stride without turning a hair, but these days—why, I feel quite jaded. Very irritating it is.

Joan You don't look—jaded.

Eva appears in the archway, glamorized with a blonde wig on and a sexy outfit: tight jeans and sweater. She stands waiting for Rex to notice her, looking at him

Joan Oh, Rex—this is my sister. Eva, this is Rex Randolph.

Rex (*with appreciation*) A sister as well! Why Joan, you never told me you had a pretty sister.

Joan She was only a little girl in those days.

Rex She's not a little girl now!

Eva So you're the famous Rex Randolph.

Rex Famous! Don't you mean notorious?

Eva Not where my sister is concerned.

Joan Eva—please.

Rex Ah well, we're old friends!

Eva So I believe!

Rex I can't get over her coming back after all this time, and remembering everything so well.

Eva She's the type who remembers things.

Rex Yes, apparently. I think this really calls for a celebration. What say we have a drink? I know it's early . . .

Eva It's never too early.
Rex Ah, a girl after my own heart.
Joan (*softly, for Eva's ears only*) As long as that's all she's after.

Eva grins at her mischievously

Rex (*going round behind the bar*) Come on then, what will it be—Eva?
Eva Scotch, please. I could do with a hair of the dog.
Joan (*muttering*) Put plenty of ice in it.
Eva (*in reply*) Miaow!
Rex (*not noticing this exchange; pouring out the drinks*) Joan—what about you?
Joan No, thank you.
Rex Oh, come on, it is a special occasion.
Joan No, really, I couldn't. Later perhaps.
Rex I'll take you up on that. Roy?
Commander No thanks, old boy. It's much too early for me.
Rex (*handing the drink to Eva*) Here's to the good old days!
Eva And the bad new ones!
Rex I'll drink to that!

They drink. Rex and Eva exchange intimate glances which do not go unnoticed by Joan

Celia enters through the archway

Celia Oh, Rex, I thought you were back. Old George wants a hand to pick the plums. You know he can't climb up ladders at his age.
Rex O.K. In a minute. What do you think, Celia, these ladies are old customers.
Celia (*sharply*) I know all about that. Isn't it rather early to be drinking?
Rex It's a special occasion. It's not every day old customers turn up out of the blue. We're lucky to have any customers at all these days.
Celia That's just as well since you're never here to look after them. Now please help old George, I don't want him walking out on us.
Rex O.K. When I've had my breakfast! (*He raises his glass to her impudently*)

Celia scowls at him, tosses her head and walks off. The Commander looks after her thoughtfully and then rises and goes out

Commander (*off*) Celia, can I help?
Rex (*waiting until he is out of earshot*) There goes old faithful!
Eva I think he's rather sweet.
Rex Like another drink?
Eva No thanks, as the lady says it is a bit early.
Rex That was no lady that was my wicked step-mother.
Eva Just like in the fairy stories.
Rex That's right.
Eva I can't believe she's wicked.

Rex Can't you?

Joan (*trying to draw his attention away from Eva*) She wasn't here before, was she?

Rex She seems always to have been here, but I suppose it was only about seven years ago that she came to work here.

Eva And then your father married her, how romantic!

Rex No, she married my father, and that wasn't romantic at all.

Eva What's the difference?

Rex A subtle one. If Joan remembers my old man as well as she remembers everything else about that holiday she'll know what I mean.

Joan I think I do.

Rex Still I suppose I'd better oblige—and pick her plums for her.

Eva I'll come too.

Rex No, you're a guest.

Eva Don't be silly, I'd like to. I want to see round the garden and I love plums.

Joan (*drily*) Since when?

Eva Just this minute!

Rex Come on then, come round this way.

He leads her round the back of the bar and they go out through the opening at the back. Joan watches them with misgiving. She sighs and goes over to the window, just as George appears

Joan Oh, I didn't see you there.

George Sorry, missus, I'm looking for that young Rex. Is he about?

Joan He's just coming to help you.

George And about time, too.

Joan With my sister.

George Ar, the pretty one that is. I knew he'd cast his eye that way soon as I saw her.

Joan (*resentfully*) Yes, she's the pretty one.

George (*realizing his tactlessness*) Handsome is as handsome does, I always say.

Joan Yes, but it usually does very well.

George Beg your pardon?

Joan Nothing—nothing important!

George (*waving his hands round his head*) Dang 'em, dang those wasps!

Joan (*concerned*) Have you been stung?

George Stung, miss, I reckon I've been stung that much I'm immuned against them now. Look at my 'ands. I 'ad one settle there this morning but I reckon his sting couldn't get through my skin, like leather it is, that's what comes of being out in all weathers, like. Some folks say as bees' stings are good for arthritis, but if it was wasps' stings then I'm dang sure I wouldn't suffer with the screws like I do. Ah, there they are coming out of the kitchen with they baskets. I'm coming—all right, 'ang on now . . .

He goes out of sight

Joan stands at the window looking out but evidently the sight is not pleasing to her and she turns round and goes down-stage

Joan (*muttering*) What a fool I am!

The Commander enters and stands looking at her. He moves down-stage

Commander Is there anything wrong?

Joan (*turning; startled*) No, no. I often talk to myself. It comes of living alone.

Commander I thought you lived with your sister.

Joan No, not really. I live in Richmond. She mostly lives in London, sharing various flats with various friends. She comes home only when she's in some sort of trouble or broke.

Commander She's a very attractive girl.

Joan Yes, that is the trouble.

Commander Oh?

Joan Well, men have always clustered around her like bees round a honey-pot. You can't blame her really.

Commander What for?

Joan For—just being herself.

Commander (*after a pause, reflectively*) I think you are beginning to regret coming back here.

Joan (*surprised*) Yes, I am.

Commander (*gently*) Forgive me for saying so, but I was in here just now when you were talking to Rex. It has been rather a sentimental journey for you, hasn't it, coming back?

Joan Yes, very much so.

Commander But have you stopped to think—I'm sorry, I don't want you to think me impertinent, after all, we've only just met.

Joan No, go on, you've aroused my curiosity now.

Commander (*with resolution*) It seems to me that the place itself, being so beautiful and old, and you having a rather romantic disposition, well, it cast a spell over you. Some places are like that. I've always thought it rather enchanted, this hotel. After all, it's five hundred years old at least, and all those years must mean something, something remains from history—the people who have lived here before.

Joan Yes, they leave an atmosphere behind, don't they? They must do.

Commander Isn't it possible, then, that it's this place you're really attached to, and the memories you had when you were here before, and that it has nothing to do with—anybody else?

Joan Have I made myself so obvious?

Commander Do tell me if you think I'm a nosey and interfering old man.

Joan I don't think any such thing. It's nice of you to be concerned. But you're wrong in your assumption. (*She turns away from him, afraid that he might see the truth in her eyes*) Rex was always very charming, of course, but I wasn't stupid enough to take him seriously.

Commander I'm glad about that, forgive me for interfering. It's the only hobby I have left now, trying to sort out other people's lives!

Joan I think you're too modest. It isn't . . .

There is a scream off L., *followed by sobbing*

Joan What on earth . . .?

Eva appears in the window sobbing and holding her cheek, followed by Rex and George

Rex She's been stung.
George Those danged wasps . . .
Joan Oh dear, come and sit down. (*She sits Eva at one of the tables*)

They gather round her. George is still outside the window

Eva I didn't see the beastly thing until it was too late. I went to eat a plum and two of them flew out and attacked me. Oh, it does hurt! It's like red hot needles.
George I'll call the missus—I thought this might happen. They don't go for me. It's people they don't know, like . . .
Rex Who'd want to go for you, George? I expect they stung Eva because they thought she was a flower.
Eva (*brightening visibly*) Oh, what a nice thing to say!
George Some people have been known to die of wasp stings, if they're allergic to 'em or something, or if they 'appen to sting 'em on the throat.
Eva Do send him away, Rex.
Rex Get my step-mother, George, will you, and tell her what's happened.
George All right, I'm going. I said it would 'appen, now didn't I? I said something would 'appen if we didn't get them plums in . . .

He disappears from view, calling out

Missus, the young 'oman's been stung bad . . .
Rex (*mimicking him as he goes*) Dang pesky things!
Eva Don't make me laugh, it hurts!
Joan Where did it sting you?
Eva In two places. (*She points to her chin*) Here and here. I went to eat a plum and out they flew, two great beastly things.
Commander I thought you got some poison for them at one time, Rex.
Rex Yes, I did, cyanide. The old boy's still got it in the shed.
Commander Why doesn't he use it?
Rex Don't ask me. You know old George. One has to keep on at him all the time.
Eva Oh dear, I shall look awful now with my face all swollen up.
Rex No, you won't. How about a drink? That should help. (*He goes behind the bar*)
Eva Oh, thank you. It would settle my nerves.
Joan (*irritably*) It was silly of you to go out there this morning. You weren't feeling your best. (*Moving away to* C.)
Eva What's that got to do with it? I suppose it's my fault I got stung!
Joan No, but . . .
Eva But what?

Celia enters through the archway R. *carrying a small bottle and cotton wool*

Celia I hear you've been stung. I'm so sorry. (*She goes to Eva by the table*) I've got some vinegar here. That will take the swelling down. (*She pours some on the cotton wool and hands it to Eva*) Or I can find some lemon juice if you prefer.

Eva Oh dear, I'm going to smell like a salad, or a fish and chip shop!

Celia Not for long! Let me see. (*She bends over her*) Well, they haven't left their stings in, that's one good thing.

Eva I'd no idea it could be so painful.

Joan Perhaps you'd better come upstairs and rest.

Eva I'd rather stay down here and rest.

Joan You look rather a mess.

Eva Oh, that's different. (*She rises*)

Rex (*going over with her drink*) Here, take it with you. I'll be up in a minute and see how you are.

Eva (*pleased*) Oh, thanks very much.

Joan and Eva go off through archway to L.

Joan You are a baby, making such a fuss.

Eva I didn't expect sympathy from *you*.

Celia (*looking after them critically*) She's quite right. What a fuss to make over a small sting!

Rex Two small stings!

Celia Even so!

Rex Ar, these city girls, like, they ain't used to country life!

Commander She'll get over it in half an hour.

Rex She'd better. We're going swimming.

Celia Rex, you can't. You've been up all night. You need some rest. I want you to be here tonight. There's that crowd coming in from the Country Club to dinner, and I must have a man to play Mine Host. You know I haven't got a wine waiter, either.

Rex Roy is very good at playing Mine Host, and you're much better at serving the wine than I am.

Celia But it isn't a woman's job.

Rex Oh, come now, in these days of unisex . . . (*He puts his arm round her teasingly*)

Celia (*pulling away from him*) Rex, you're so infuriating. Where were you last night anyway? Gambling again, I suppose?

Rex A little.

Celia And losing.

Rex No, actually, I won.

Celia That's a change. Then you can remember to pay for your drinks today. Drinking on the house means me, you know.

Rex O.K. Look! That's for those drinks I had this morning. (*He goes behind the bar and puts a pound note in the till*) Satisfied?

Celia For the time being, but it isn't fair. You just can't go on like this.

Rex Why not?

Celia It isn't fair.

Rex Nothing is ever fair. How naïve you are if you think it should be. (*Pouring himself another drink*) I might as well have another one to make up that pound. Care to join me?

Celia No, I wouldn't. I've got far too much to do. (*She goes furiously towards the archway and then stops, relenting a little, her tone more pleading than angry*) I'm sorry, Rex. I don't mean to be hard on you, but I wish you'd try to understand my point of view. We are running a business here. We can't just live for pleasure, either of us.

Rex Why not? We're a long time dead. (*He looks at her insolently across the bar*) What else is there to live for but pleasure?

Celia I wish you'd try to understand.

Rex I am trying.

Celia (*wearily*) All you're trying is my patience!

She goes off through the archway to the L.

Rex (*looking after her with a shrug and then turning to Roy*) Care to join me?

Commander No thanks.

Rex (*coming round the bar with his drink*) I'm surprised I haven't had your opinion of my behaviour. (*He sits in the armchair*)

Commander It's none of my business.

Rex No, but you usually make it your business.

Commander If you really want to know . . .

Rex I don't, but tell me anyway.

Commander I'm very worried about Celia. She doesn't look well, and she tells me she's been sleeping badly. Something will happen. She can't go on like this.

Rex Like what?

Commander Propping *you* up.

Rex This is my home. It always has been. *She*'s the interloper, not I.

Commander But it isn't just a home, is it? It's a business. Your father realized that. He knew you couldn't take a living out and put nothing back. That's why he left the business in Celia's hands, and not yours. He knew she could be trusted with it.

Rex And I cannot?

Commander Isn't that obvious?

Rex (*irritably*) It hasn't occurred to anybody, has it, that if I were given a bit more responsibility I might be more responsible?

Commander It's a big risk to take.

Rex Naturally, you're on Celia's side. You always have been.

Commander It's not a question of sides . . .

Rex What's your solution to it all then?

Commander I haven't one. I'm an outsider. I shall simply wait and observe and be around to pick up the pieces when Celia needs me—like when the hotel is auctioned under her feet to pay your debts.

Rex It certainly won't come to that. I'll get by. I always have. I rely on my charm.

Commander You rely rather too heavily on your charm, if I might say so. It doesn't put money in the bank.

Rex (*amused*) It could do—if I met a rich old millionairess!
Commander They're rather few and far between.
Rex (*musing*) Pity the little school-teacher isn't rich.
Commander Why do you say that?
Rex She's obviously taken with me.
Commander You could always be wrong.
Rex No, I know. I can tell. That bright look in her eyes, she fancies me all right.
Commander (*tartly*) I thought she was a very sensible person.
Rex (*ignoring this; smiling*) Funny thing, though.
Commander What is?
Rex She remembers that holiday of hers down to the minutest details, whereas I . . .
Commander Yes?
Rex I don't remember a thing. (*He laughs*) Angela told me her name, and I played along. I actually can't remember her at all.
Commander I see.
Rex Pity she isn't rich!

He looks thoughtfully at the Commander, then shrugs and turns away, sipping his drink. The Commander looks at him with cold dislike as—

the CURTAIN *falls*

SCENE 2

The same. Evening, after dinner, two days later

The curtains are drawn at the windows and the wall lights are on. Joan is sitting in the armchair L.C. *wearing a long dress. There is a coffee cup on the table beside her. "Love Walked In" is just coming to an end in the record-player. Some old records are scattered on the table and floor*

Angela enters from the archway

Angela (*above the music*) Did you want any more coffee, miss?
Joan No, thank you. That was delicious.
Angela I'll take your cup then. I'm off this evening, you see.
Joan Yes, all right. (*She rises and goes over to the record-player as the record comes to an end and turns it off*)
Angela (*coming over to take the coffee cup*) You like that tune, don't you, miss?
Joan Yes, very much. Just for sentimental reasons. We used to play it a lot when I stayed here before.
Angela Sounds as if it's come out of the Ark to me!
Joan Yes, I know it's old. It was old ten years ago, but I still like it. It was a great favourite of the old Mr Randolph, you know. Rex was kind enough to find these records for me—up in the attic or somewhere like that.

Angela He can be—very obliging when he tries. (*She looks over her shoulder to make sure they are not being overheard, and then turns back to Joan confidentially*) Missus is in a fair state about him being out all day again.

Joan Mm, yes. He went to Brighton with my sister.

Angela And all day yesterday they was out, wasn't they? Littlehampton, or somewhere.

Joan Yes—somewhere . . .

Angela Missus says it's all very well, but he can't go on behaving as if he's on holiday too. I mean to say, it's lonely for you as well!

Joan (*tartly*) I'm used to it.

Angela (*after a pause, nervously*) I thought I ought to tell you . . .

Joan (*irritably*) Tell me what?

Angela This morning, quite late on, I took Rex a cup of tea in his room, on account of the missus was gettin' so cross about him not being up . . .

Joan Well?

Angela Your sister's wig—it was on his bedside table, like. I took it up right away and hid it in a drawer. I could 'ear the missus outside, you see . . . and then afterwards when they'd gone out I went back and put it in her room.

Joan (*sharply, trying to hide her chagrin*) Thank you very much, but you shouldn't have taken so much trouble. It didn't mean anything just finding her wig. She's careless about where she leaves it . . . (*She breaks off, avoiding Angela's knowing eyes*)

Angela The missus, though, you see, she gets very jealous about his carryings-on.

Joan I'm sure he isn't . . . I mean, it's nobody's business, is it?

Angela The missus always makes it her business. Like the time he took off with the barmaid from "The Plough" down in the village.

Joan What do you mean—took off?

Angela Went away with her he did, for a whole week. Missus fixed him that time, though.

Joan How?

Angela Took an overdose that's how. He soon came running back.

Joan (*surprised*) Are you sure? I thought she would be glad to see the back of him the way she complains.

Angela I'm sure. She made no secret of it. She wanted him to know so that he'd feel guilty and come back.

Joan She behaves more like a possessive wife . . . (*She breaks off, realizing what she has said*)

Angela (*significantly*) Others have said that, miss—very possessive she is.

There is a pause, while the two women exchange glances, Joan puzzled, Angela smug

Angela There's been a lot of funny talk . . .

Joan So you said . . .

Angela About the way the old man died.

Joan (*uneasily*) Oh yes?

Angela Them just being married a few months and 'im popping off like that—funny it was.

Joan He *was* an old man.

Angela Yes, but he went so sudden, like, took everyone by surprise.

Joan Was it a heart attack?

Angela Yes. Mind you, he'd suffered with his 'eart for years, and he had some sort of medication, but I reckon he never took it regular—that's what old George says anyhow.

Joan I don't really think we should be discussing this . . .

Angela (*as if Joan hasn't spoken*) Mind you, they both have such a collection of medicines up there, it's not surprising if he got them muddled up . . .

Joan What do you mean—where?

Angela Up in their bedrooms, the master and missus. They used to 'ave separate rooms, you see, but they both had a collection of bottles by their bedside. *She* still has. Sleeping pills and slimming pills and goodness knows what clse. 'Tisn't natural, my mother says, to depend that much on pills.

Joan We all do nowadays to a certain extent.

Angela 'Tisn't natural, though, is it?

Joan (*reprovingly*) I really do think, Angela, that all this is none of our business.

Celia (*off, calling*) Angela . . .

Angela (*in some panic*) Oh, God—don't tell 'er, will you, what I've been saying?

Joan shakes her head reassuringly just as Celia appears in the bar entrance. She is in evening dress but looks very cross

Celia Angela, your boyfriend is waiting for you right outside the front door, with his motor bike. I do wish you'd tell him not to bring that nasty, noisy thing right down the drive. He should leave it by the gate and walk up.

Angela Yes, missus, I'll tell him. Sorry, I was just collecting the coffee cup like. I'm off now.

She exits through the archway

(*calling*) Good night!

Joan Good night. (*She picks up the records and begins to go through them*)

Celia Really, that girl at times! Would you care for a drink? (*She pours herself a gin and tonic*)

Joan No, thank you.

Celia It's so difficult to get good staff in the country. It doesn't seem to matter what you pay. Rex is no help at all.

Joan (*drily*) I had noticed.

There is a pause

Celia As a matter of fact I'm rather glad to find you alone. I wanted to have a word with you,

Joan (*unhelpfully*) Oh?
Celia After all, you're not just a guest, are you? You're an old friend.
Joan I like to think so.
Celia (*coming round the bar*) It's about Rex.
Joan What about him?
Celia You must know what a trial he is to me.
Joan It isn't any of my business.
Celia You knew him a long time ago.
Joan (*moving away across the stage; evasively*) It still isn't any of my business.
Celia (*pettishly*) Your sister—I suppose she's your business?
Joan (*after a pause*) My sister is—should be capable of looking after herself.
Celia Ah yes, should be, but she isn't is she? Neither is Rex. They are two thoroughly weak and hopeless people.
Joan (*reluctantly*) That's true. Perhaps they deserve one another.
Celia You don't understand, I'm concerned about both of them. He's useless without me behind him. He needs a strong woman. And he hasn't any money of his own. His father made sure of that. Everything is in my name for as long as I live and I'm not all that old. (*Becoming agitated*) Don't you see, his father knew what he was like. He made sure he wouldn't have control of the money. He can't be trusted with it. I wouldn't worry but with your sister being an heiress—
Joan (*amazed*) A what?
Celia An heiress—isn't she? She told Rex she comes into a small fortune when she's twenty-one, some distant relative who favours her apparently and not you.
Joan (*almost laughing*) Oh, clever little Eva. That was one way to retain his interest I suppose.
Celia Then she isn't an heiress?
Joan All that girl is heiress to is my pension and that will be little enough, I can tell you.
Celia (*relieved*) Neither of you have any money?
Joan Not enough to worry about. Not enough to interest Rex, I'm afraid.
Celia You do understand him, don't you?
Joan Only too well.
Celia Then why should she lie?
Joan (*ruefully*) My sister always lies. She has lied habitually since she was a small child. She must get her own way, you see, and she doesn't care how she does it.
Celia I suppose she isn't a fashion model either?
Joan Oh really!
Celia Yes, I thought that was stretching it a bit. She has to make her life more glamorous, I suppose.
Joan I don't believe she thinks about it consciously. She doesn't seem to know the difference. As soon as she's uttered it, her lie becomes the truth to her, until she thinks of another lie. She's a hopeless case, I'm afraid.
Celia (*sympathetically*) She must be quite a worry to you.

Joan She is. It's strange, isn't it, how different we are? You'd hardly think we were sisters. She's never stayed in any job for more than a few weeks at a time. I don't know what she'd do without me to look after her.

Celia What about your parents?

Joan They died within a few months of each other five years ago. They left me with a large house—and Eva.

Celia (*sympathetically*) We're rather alike, aren't we? We've both had responsibility thrust upon us.

Joan Strong people always do.

Celia While the weak just indulge themselves at our expense.

Joan (*ruefully*) Yes, but I envy them in a way, don't you?

Celia Not at all. What would the world be like if we all behaved like that.

Joan That's the age-old cry.

Celia (*abruptly*) I don't intend to let him go, you know.

Joan Who?

Celia (*snapping*) Rex, of course.

Joan Don't worry about it. I'll take Eva away. It's for her own good.

Celia (*relieved*) I'm glad you understand.

The women look at one another in apparent mutual sympathy

The Commander comes through the archway and stands looking at them

Commander Oh, am I interrupting a *tête-à-tête*?

Celia Not at all. Come and have a drink. I need cheering up. Perhaps you'll join us—Joan?

Joan No thank you. I think it might be an idea if I packed.

Commander Are you leaving us?

Joan I think it might be best.

She nods at them both politely and exits through the archway to the L.

Commander (*going round behind the bar to pour himself a drink*) Whatever you say, I still think I was interrupting something.

Celia No, not really. We had been talking, but we'd finished.

Commander I won't ask what it was about because I can guess. Do you want another drink?

Celia (*going up to the bar with her glass*) Yes, please, gin. What was it about, since you know me so well?

Commander (*pouring her a drink*) The miscreant Rex, of course.

Celia Of course. (*She takes the drink and sips it absently*) How did you guess?

Commander (*pouring himself a Scotch, and then carefully putting the money in the till*) One doesn't have to be a detective to figure out the big pre-occupation of your life.

Celia He isn't a preoccupation, he's a worry.

Commander Then he shouldn't be.

Celia He's my responsibility.

Commander (*coming round the bar to her; very firmly*) He isn't your responsibility at all. He's your step-son and he's more than thirty years old, and even if he were your real son he should be standing on his own feet by now.

Celia But he can't.

Commander He can, if you let him.

Celia How? He's just as much a legacy from his father as this hotel.

Commander Then get rid of both of them.

Celia I couldn't. What do you mean?

Commander Sell up. Give him his share and quit.

Celia Quit?

Commander Of course, why not? This place is too much for you. He won't pull his weight, so just cut loose and let him have his head.

Celia It isn't what his father would want.

Commander (*with studied patience*) Celia, I've known you a long time. You're not staying on here out of some sense of loyalty to your dead husband.

Celia I'm not?

Commander No.

Celia (*warily*) Then why am I staying on?

Commander (*uneasily*) I know I'm interfering—

Celia Yes, you are.

Commander But as an old friend I think I have a right to—

Celia Why?

Commander I've known you a long time—

Celia Don't presume too much on that!

Commander (*persuasively, trying another tactic*) Do you remember when we first met?

Celia Yes, of course I do. In Hong Kong. How could I forget?

Commander Do you think our relationship meant nothing to me?

Celia I don't know. It couldn't mean much. *You* were married.

Commander I'm not now.

Celia It's too late now. Much too late.

Commander Why? I know I'm a good bit older than you, but so was your first husband.

Celia It's not that.

Commander Since I've retired and come down here I've been happy, Celia. For the first time for years I haven't been lonely. It was only the other day that I realized why. You know, it's pretty unusual to admit to being happy. Happiness is a state of mind one aspires to, or looks back on but actually to say "Now I'm happy" that's unusual!

Celia (*impatiently*) Is it? I'm sorry, Roy, I don't know what you're getting at. I have some things to do . . . (*She moves towards the archway*)

Commander (*calling her back*) Let me help you!

Celia (*apprehensively*) How? I don't know what you mean.

Commander Let me help you face reality.

Celia Don't be obtuse. I know what reality is all about.

Commander Not the reality of your own emotions. I know what's bothering you. Believe me, it would be easier shared.

Celia (*warily*) What would? I don't understand you. Please leave me alone.

Commander (*gently*) You don't want me to cross the ts and dot the is, do you?

Celia I don't want you to do anything. I have to go.

Commander I'm not afraid of offending you. I've known you too long for that.

Celia Drop it! (*In sudden panic, knowing what is coming*) Leave me alone!

Commander Other women have fallen in love with their step-sons, it's nothing to be ashamed of.

Celia (*furiously*) How dare you? (*She goes to slap his face*)

Commander (*taking hold of her hands, still gentle*) Deny it then.

Celia (*she struggles to be free and then suddenly collapses against him weeping*) Oh Roy, I'm so ashamed, so ashamed . . .

Commander There, cry it out, you'll feel better afterwards. (*He holds her gently while she sobs on his shoulder*)

Celia I'm such a fool—such an old fool—I didn't realize it was happening, not at first, not until I got jealous of him. Oh, Roy, it's been such agony. I hate every girl he looks at—the thought of him touching them—all those other women. Oh Roy, how can I get over it? How can I?

Commander I assure you, you can.

Celia But how—how? I've tried.

Commander You've tried alone. But now you have me to help you.

Celia (*straightening up, and finding a handkerchief in her evening bag*) Oh Roy. You must think me such a fool! (*She blows her nose and wipes her eyes*) It's such a relief, that somebody knows . . .

Commander I've known for months. I wasn't sure what to do about it. But when this girl came here and they were so obviously carrying on under your nose I knew you wouldn't be able to stand any more, so I thought it was time you faced facts.

Celia Yes, you're right. You're so right. I feel better already. (*Shamefacedly*) It isn't all that terrible, is it? I hate you knowing about it.

Commander My dear woman, it isn't terrible at all. Some women are in love with their own sons all their lives and never face the fact. Rex isn't your real son, and he's very attractive. I doubt whether any woman could live in close proximity with him for long without becoming a victim to his numerous charms, particularly when, like you, she hasn't anyone else to love.

Celia You understand! You're so good to me.

Commander No, I'm not. I'm as self-seeking as any other man. My help isn't entirely disinterested.

Celia (*puzzled*) It isn't?

Commander Of course not. I shall be on the look out for my reward!

Celia (*laughing, despite herself, and bending over to kiss him on the cheek*) Oh Roy, you're my very best friend, always, you know that—

There is the sound of a car approaching. Celia looks round towards the windows

Oh dear, it must be them. I look a mess. (*She goes towards the archway*)

I'll remember your advice, Roy, honestly. From now on I'll be a different person.

Commander Not too different, I hope!

She smiles at him affectionately as she goes through the archway to the L.

The Commander looks after her thoughtfully and then goes to the window, and lifts the curtain, looking out. He turns back into the room, frowning. Voices can be heard off R. of the archway

Eva (*off*) The trouble with most drivers is they take the lay in lay-by too literally.

Rex Only if you look the type, men aren't that stupid!

They both come into the room

Oh hallo, Roy . . .

Commander Good evening. Nice of you to come back!

Rex We had to, really. I ran out of money. (*He goes round behind the bar*) Let's have a drink. Roy?

Commander (*stiffly*) No, I'm all right, thank you.

Rex I wonder why people say they're all right when they don't want a drink. I know you're all right, but do you want a drink?

Commander I already have one. (*He lifts his glass to Rex*)

Rex Ah yes—(*as he pours himself a Scotch*)—a snifter for you poppet?

Eva Anything will do—to top me up! (*She sits on the bar stool, after one or two attempts*)

Rex pours her a drink. He raises his glass to her and they drink, looking into one another's eyes

Commander (*watching them with some irritation*) How did you find Brighton?

Rex Why, we just drove along the road and there it was!

Eva giggles appreciatively

Commander I see. I won't bore you with my company. You obviously have other things on your mind. (*He finishes his drink and puts down the glass on the table by the window*) I think I'll go for a stroll. I feel like a breath of fresh air.

He goes through the french windows, pulling the curtains closed behind him

Eva What's he so po-faced about?

Rex They get like that when I take a day off.

Eva Anyone would think he was your father.

Rex He'd like to be—at least he'd like to be my step-father, I think.

Eva Oh, does he fancy Celia?

Rex Well, she's not bad, is she, for her age? He's known her for yonks. I don't know why he didn't pop the question before.

Eva Perhaps he did, only not the question you mean. (*She giggles*)

Rex (*also laughing*) You think everybody is as sex-mad as you are!

Eva They'd like to be. They just haven't got the guts, most of them. I behave the way other people want to behave, that's why they hate me. I'm all id.

Rex What's that?

Eva You know, the primitive part of your personality. Surely you've read Freud?

Rex No, have you?

Eva Not really. I couldn't understand it. (*Sliding off the stool, and holding on to the bar for support*) Christ, I feel stoned! Do you realize we haven't stopped drinking since yesterday lunch-time!

Rex Except when we were in bed!

Eva (*giggling*) Oh yes, I'd forgotten. Have I said thank you?

Rex I'll take it as said!

Eva (*swaying towards the archway*) I must have a rest though, before tonight.

Rex It already is tonight.

Eva (*looking at him over her shoulder*) I mean before tonight is over.

Rex Oh yes, quite. Suits me!

He raises his glass to her as she goes out. Then he finishes his drink and pours himself another one. Celia enters through the back of the bar and stands watching him

Celia Are you paying for that?

Rex Of course. (*He fumbles in his pocket for some money*) I seem to be a bit short of change.

Celia That girl is drunk.

Rex Which girl?

Celia The girl who's just passed me in the hall.

Rex Oh, *that* girl.

Celia She smelled like a barrack room.

Rex You have the advantage over me there, Celia. I don't know what a barrack room smells like.

Celia I've had enough, Rex. I'd just like you to know.

Rex I'm getting the drift.

Celia Roy has given me some very good advice tonight, and I've a damned good mind to take it.

Rex What was it, go jump in the lake?

Celia (*after a pause, simply and without anger*) You really don't care about me at all, do you? You really don't care about anyone except yourself. I don't know why it's taken me so long to realize it.

Rex Does it matter?

Celia Apparently not. (*She sighs and puts her hand to her head*) I think I'll go to bed early. My head aches.

Rex Why don't you do that sweet thing? (*He finishes his drink and defiantly pours himself another one*)

Celia (*with a withering look at him*) Good night.

She goes out through the back of the bar

Rex Good night, darling! Sleep tight! (*He raises his glass to her retreating back. He sighs to himself; muttering*) Oh, Christ! (*He shrugs and wanders round the front of the bar. He is a little unsteady on his feet and grips the bar. Then he goes down-stage to the record-player and putting his drink down begins to look through the records*)

Joan enters. Rex does not see her at first. She stands looking at him, her face clearly revealing her feelings

Joan You're back then.

Rex Oh yes. (*He turns to look at her*) You *are* observant!

Joan I thought I heard Eva in her room.

Rex Yes, she went upstairs to rest. She's feeling like me, a bit under the weather.

Joan Oh, I see. (*She moves to him*) I was playing one of those old seventy-eights earlier on. I hope you don't mind.

Rex Of course not. I brought them down here for you.

Joan (*abruptly*) I've decided to go home tomorrow.

Rex (*surprised*) Why?

Joan (*confused*) I just don't seem to be enjoying myself . . . besides I've got a lot to do before the term starts and that's only next week.

Rex I see. What about Eva?

Joan She'll have to come with me, of course.

Rex Why?

Joan She hasn't any money of her own.

Rex Perhaps we could find her a job. She isn't working at the moment.

Joan (*shortly*) No, she doesn't believe in working if she can avoid it.

Rex We could find her something to do—stand around and look decorative, that would be enough.

Joan I doubt whether your step-mother would agree.

Rex Oh, I can get round *her*.

Joan You take an awful lot for granted, Rex.

Rex (*complacently*) I've always got my own way, sooner or later.

Joan There's bound to be a day of reckoning.

Rex There speaks a good little puritan! I thought you'd been around long enough to know that virtue is its own reward and the wicked always prosper.

Joan I didn't notice you were prospering, if you include yourself in the latter category.

Rex No, I'm not. (*Thoughtfully*) As a matter of fact I'm skint. I suppose you couldn't do me a favour before you leave, and lend me a few quid?

Joan Oh really, Rex! (*She is amused at his audacity*) You are the giddy limit!

Rex Am I? (*He goes over to her, smiling*) You know I've never forgotten you, Joan, not for an instance.

Joan Then why didn't you write to me? Ten years is a long time.

Rex I meant to at first, but I kept putting it off. I was afraid of getting too serious. After all, what did I have to offer a girl in those days?

Joan What have you got now?

Rex Yes, exactly. You understand, don't you? I mean, there must have been other men in your life.

Joan One or two, but you see I could never get you out of my mind.

Rex (*pleased*) Really?

Joan (*ruefully*) I'm afraid so. I kept searching for someone else like you. I must have been a very silly and impressionable young girl.

Rex Oh, I wouldn't say that.

Joan I came back partly out of curiosity.

Rex I wondered.

Joan I feel better now.

> *Unseen by them the Commander crosses from* R. *to* L. *across the archway, stopping briefly to glance at them*

Rex You do?

Joan Yes, I've laid the ghost.

Rex I'm not sure I like to be referred to as a ghost and I can't remember being laid.

Joan (*softly and thoughtfully*) No, I thought you couldn't.

Rex (*catching her mood, also softly*) I'm sorry.

> *He looks as if he is going to kiss her, and she is quite willing, when Eva and the Commander appear in the archway. Joan and Rex break apart; he to the bar, she down-stage* R.

> *Eva is more drunk than ever and very giggly. She is wearing her wig and has changed her clothes*

Eva Look what I found on the stairs!

Commander Bumped into would be more accurate.

Rex I thought you'd gone to bed.

Eva No, I decided to change and keep going. I feel revved up, I don't want my motor to stop.

Rex Another little drinkie?

Eva (*singing*) Wouldn't do us any harm!

Rex (*he pours her a large Scotch and one for himself*) Commander?

Commander Yes, I'll join you this time. (*He looks anxiously at Joan*) What about you, Joan?

Joan No, thanks. I'm not in the mood.

Eva (*going over to her; swaying*) Oh, but you must.

Joan (*tensely*) Why, must I?

Eva Because it's a little celebration, that's why.

Joan What exactly are we supposed to be celebrating?

Eva Oh, hasn't Rexy told you? Naughty Rexy! (*She floats back over to him*) My darling, sexy Rexy, Randy Randolph . . . (*She giggles*) That's what they called him at school, you know, isn't it apt?

Commander Really Rex? I didn't realize you went to school?

Rex Where do you think I learned to be a cad, you rotter? Oh come on, Joan, have a drink, don't be such an old misery.

Joan I'm not—

Eva You should be very pleased to get your sister off your hands.

Joan (*worried now*) What do you mean?
Eva Only that Rex and I are going to get married, that's all!
Joan (*horrified*) What? You can't! You just can't!
Eva Why not? There's nothing to stop us except for Rex's wicked old step-mother, and we'll soon get rid of her.
Rex Shut up, Eva. Darling, you're a bit too pickled.
Commander Is it true?
Rex Oh, God! Who knows? We discussed it.
Eva Of course it's true. I won't let you get out of it now. Look, in front of witnesses. Anyway, you've got to marry me now you've ruined me. (*She giggles*)
Rex Christ, that's rich! I'd like a pound for every man who'd ruined *you*, my girl!
Eva So would I!
Commander Be sensible for a minute, Rex. Is she telling the truth?
Rex (*evasively*) More or less.
Commander Then may I be the first to congratulate you? If ever two people deserved one another, you do. (*He goes to Joan with a drink and gives it to her*) Come on, Joan, let's drink their health. (*He is solicitous, admonishing her with his eyes not to give in*)
Joan (*tense and unhappy, but making an effort*) Yes, of course—to the happy couple. (*She forces the drink down and shudders*)
Eva There, you see! I told you she'd be glad to get rid of me. Now I'm your responsibility.
Rex God help me!

Rex leans across the bar and kisses Eva. The Commander and Joan watch uneasily

Celia appears in the archway in her négligé and carrying a bottle of capsules. She glares at Rex and Eva

Celia (*irritably*) That girl forgot to leave any water by my bedside. And she moved my sleeping-pills. I don't know what's come over her.
Rex (*breaking away from Eva, somewhat guiltily*) Oh, bad show! Have a drink. (*He goes to pour her a gin*)
Celia I don't want a drink. Unlike you I know when I've had enough. Some water will do.
Rex Righto! (*He pours her some water from a jug on the bar*)
Celia (*sourly*) You seem to be enjoying yourselves. I'm sorry to interrupt you.
Eva (*giggling*) We're celebrating!
Celia What? Is Rex going to work?
Rex Now, now, don't be bitchy, dear. You should be pleased to see me back.
Celia I'd rather see the back of you.
Eva That's a fine way to talk. This is *his* hotel, you know, not yours!
Rex (*instantly*) Shut up, Eva!
Celia You know nothing about it!
Eva Oh, yes, I do! We'll fight you for it.

Celia (*puzzled*) What are you talking about?

Joan (*conciliatory*) I'm afraid she's rather drunk, Celia, please don't take any notice.

Eva I'm not drunk! I'm not a bit drunk.

Celia (*icily*) Perhaps you can explain what she means, Rex.

Rex (*evasively*) I really don't know.

Eva (*surprised*) Well, you coward!

Commander (*going over to Celia*) Let it go, Celia. We'll talk about it tomorrow.

Celia I seem to have forgotten all your good advice, Roy. I'm hopeless, aren't I? (*She sighs and unscrewing the bottle, takes out a capsule*) I want to be sure of a night's rest, though. I don't seem to be able to sleep unaided these days. (*She takes a capsule washed down with the water*)

Commander You should try. It really isn't good for you.

Celia I know, I know. To be quite honest I feel like taking the whole bloody lot. (*She throws the bottle down on the bar and goes towards the archway*)

Rex (*trying to please*) I do wish you wouldn't take offence so easily, darling. I don't mean any harm.

Celia No. You never *mean* any harm. That makes it worse somehow. I'd find it easier to forgive you if it was all quite deliberate. (*She stops wearily in the archway*) Please let me sleep late tomorrow. I need the rest.

She exits L.

There is a pause

Eva (*sulkily*) Why didn't you tell her? I thought you had more courage.

Rex It didn't seem the right time.

Eva When is—the right time?

Rex Tomorrow, perhaps.

Eva (*with determination*) I shall tell her, if you don't.

Rex (*exasperatedly*) No, Eva, it isn't your place.

Eva Oh, to hell with that.

There is a strangled scream off L. followed by sobbing noises. They all look towards the archway

Joan What's that?

Celia appears in the archway clutching her throat. She looks at them all in agony and the– collapses on the floor. The Commander goes to her at once. Rex comes round the bar. Eva and Joan stand transfixed

Eva What's happened? What's going on?

Rex Celia, are you ill?

Commander (*leaning over her and taking her pulse*) Celia—Celia . . .!

Rex What is it, Roy? What's happened?

Commander (*gravely; looking at Rex*) I'm sorry Rex. She's dead!

Quick CURTAIN

ACT II

SCENE 1

One week later. Midday

Angela is behind the bar, washing up glasses. She looks worried and preoccupied. George Carter comes to the french windows, which are closed, and taps gently. She looks up startled and then she goes over with an impatient gesture and opens them

Angela What do you want? I was just tidying up the bar. They must have all had a drink before they left and the glasses was just left out for me to clear. Dutch courage, I suppose!

George That's what I was wondering about. They back yet?

Angela No, but they won't be long, I reckon. They left at ten o'clock.

George Still, it's half-an-hour's drive into Lewes, isn't it? Wonder if they keep 'em hanging about at an inquest, like at hospital, or whether it's all cut and dried and over in a jiffy.

Angela I wouldn't know.

George No more would I. I never went to an inquest. I thought they might've called me to this one, but they didn't.

Angela They didn't call me neither. I don't see that it matters. We weren't 'ere that night anyway.

George *You* wasn't mebbe. (*He grins at her*)

Angela Neither was you. You don't do your gardening in the dark, do you?

George No, not my gardening, I don't. Go down to the pub though every night around nine o'clock. Leave my cottage and walk down that twisty path, down past the garden shed.

Angela So what? I don't know why you're being so mysterious. I'm busy I am. (*She continues to tidy up the bar*)

George (*piqued*) All right, if you're not interested, it don't matter. I've got my audience down the pub.

Angela Yes, I'll bet you 'ave. I bet you've had many a pint bought you this week on the strength of what you think you know.

George What I do know is more to the point. After all, it's not every day we 'ave a suicide in the village.

Angela Ghoulish you are, George Carter, that's what. You ought to be ashamed.

George And the police, now, they was a lot more interested in my garden shed than what you are, I can tell you.

Angela (*puzzled*) Why should they be?

George (*triumphantly*) Because that's where she got it from, that's why.

Angela Got what? What do you mean?

George The poison, of course.

Angela (*surprised*) What poison? I thought the missus took an overdose or something, like last time.

George (*pleased that he knows more than she does*) Reckon not. Reckon it was cyanide, the questions they was asking me about the stuff.

Angela How awful!

George Why, death's death, isn't it, whatever way you choose?

Angela But that way—it's so painful—

George Don't know. Don't know no-one who's died of it, like, and then come back and told us. (*He chuckles*) Leastways, it's quick!

Angela (*disapproving*) You're callous, you are, George Carter, with the missus only dead a week, and by her own hand, too. It's wicked, talkin' like that.

George Ar, mebbe so. Only when you've lived as long as I 'ave death's got its funny side, like. (*Ruminatively; scratching his head*) Mate of mine once 'ad to go and shave a corpse, like, before they laid 'im out. 'Is relatives wanted 'im looking all ship-shape, the way they do. Well, the corpse was sittin' up in a chair, and my mate laid a 'and on his chest, and blow me if the dead man didn't belch in his face. (*He laughs*) Fair shook my mate, it did. Came in the pub and told us, with his face as white as parchment and 'is hands shakin' like he had the palsy. Gave us a good laugh that did. Course it was only gasses or somethin' accumulated inside, like, must 'ave been.

Angela I wish you'd shut up!

George (*grinning; deliberately taunting her*) Why, got the jitters 'ave you?

Angela Well, it's upsetting, the missus dyin' like that, so sudden, so awful.

George Suicide. I never would've thought it of her, I must say. Besides, I could've stopped it, if I'd only known.

Angela 'Ow could you? You could have been a sight more careful with that poison, I must say.

George Yes, that's true. He was right snotty about it, that Inspector fellow. "Did you sign for it, my man?" he said. "No," I said, "I never did sign for it, but that's because I never got it. It was young Mr Rex who got it." "Oh, that's different," he said. "Still, you should've kept it under lock and key." "Course," I said. "I know that now, but that's like locking the stable door when the 'orse's gone." He didn't say nothing after that. Reckon he knew it weren't my fault. I mean 'ow was I to know the missus would up and poison 'erself with it? Wasn't my fault.

Angela Then why do you say you could've stopped it? How could you?

George Well, that's just it, that's the other thing.

Angela What other thing? You are irritating tonight.

George I saw someone down there that night. (*He lowers his voice to a hoarse whisper*).

Angela Where? Who?

George In the shed. When I was on my way to the pub. I saw someone movin' about in there. I never thought no more about it. I mean there was nothin' there worth botherin' about. It's not like the greenhouse, is it? I would've been round there soon enough if it had've been the green-house with all my potted plants I've got in there. But the garden shed—Well, what did it matter?

Angela (*curiously*) Who did you see exactly?

George Better to say, what, wouldn't it? (*He grins at her impishly*) Could've been a ghost for all I know. I mean, this place is old enough to have a few.

Angela (*sharply*) Stop it! I don't hold with such talk. It's against God, my mum says, and she ought to know.

George Ar, reckon so. (*He turns to go*) I won't bother to tell you then.

Angela (*calling him back*) No, no, I want to know. Was it the missus you saw?

George Now, was it, or was it not? (*He teases her*) One thing, I wouldn't go investigatin' now if I saw somethin' down there in the gloamin'. Oh no, not I.

Angela Why not? Don't be so aggravatin', George Carter.

George Well, suicides! Now that's one sort of spirit that does roam about, so I've 'eard tell. I wouldn't go a lookin' for it, I can tell you, and I'm no coward.

Angela (*her voice sharp with a touch of hysteria*) I told you to stop that talk!

George Listen!

He holds his head to one side. They both listen intently

Reckon I 'eard somethin' then, didn't you?

There is the sound of a car approaching and drawing to a halt

Angela (*with relief*) It's them—back from the inquest. You clear off, you wicked old reprobate, frightenin' me like that.

George disappears from the window. The Commander and Joan enter, both looking rather subdued

Angela (*embarrassed, not knowing what to say*) You're back then?

Commander Yes, we're back.

Angila Everything go all right, like?

Commander Yes, of course.

Angela Perhaps you'd like a drink?

Commander I'll see to it. (*He goes behind the bar*) It's all right, Angela, We'll ring if we want something.

Angela (*taking the hint*) Oh yes, of course. I'll get on with the lunch. Something light. I didn't think you'd be hungry.

Joan I don't think I could face food at all at the moment.

Commander Nor I. You go, if you want to, Angela. We can look after ourselves.

Angela Oh, all right. (*She hovers in the bar exit*)

Commander What would you like, Joan?

Joan A stiff Scotch I think would be in order.

Commander I agree. (*He pours them both a drink, and then notices that*

Angela is still there. He turns to her a little irritably) Was there anything else, Angela?

Angela Well— no—I mean, yes. I suppose I ought to tell you, really.

Joan *(with interest)* Tell us what?

Angela *(nervously)* Just after you left, why you'd 'ardly got out of sight I'm surprised you didn't see them.

Commander See who? Spit it out, girl!

Angela The police. You'd no sooner left than they was here, three of 'em, two in civvies and the other one in uniform. 'E was the driver, the one in uniform. *(She comes down-stage)*

Joan *(apprehensively)* What did they want?

Angela They had a search warrant. All legal it was, they showed me.

Commander A search warrant?

Angela That's right. I went with them and they went through all the rooms —that is, the rooms that have been occupied.

Joan *(sharply)* Our rooms?

Angela Yes, miss.

Joan What a nerve without asking us! Roy, what do you make of it?

Commander A deliberate tactic, I'd say. They knew we'd be at the inquest, and they wanted to search the place without any fuss.

Joan Can they do that?

Commander Of course, if they have a search warrant, they certainly don't need our permission.

Joan *(crossly)* Oh, really, it's like a police state!

Commander *(smoothly)* Not quite, my dear! They still don't arrest people without evidence or hold them without trial.

Joan But why should they want to arrest anybody? How dare they treat us like common criminals?

Commander *(he looks at her thoughtfully)* Is that all, Angela, or have you anything else to tell us?

Angela No, that's all.

Joan When they left—the police—did they take anything with them?

Angela *(uneasily)* Mm, yes, I think they did.

Joan What?

Angela Some pills, they found them in Miss Eva's room, like.

Joan Pills?

Angela Yes, that's right, in a little bottle. They said they had to take them for to be analysed, I think that was the word, and then they'd bring 'em back, that's what they said.

Joan *(furiously)* Really, this is insufferable!

Commander *(soothingly)* Have a drink. It will calm your nerves.

Angela *(suddenly, blurting it out)* I'd like to know, sir . . .

Commander *(impatiently)* What?

Angela I'd like to know what they said at the inquest. That George Carter has fair put the wind up me. I'd like to know what they said.

Commander *(after a pause)* The inquest was adjourned, Angela.

Angela *(puzzled)* What does that mean?

Commander It means that they are not yet satisfied—exactly how she died.

Angela But the means, the cause of it?
Commander (*with a brief look at Joan*) Cyanide poisoning.
Angela (*shocked*) Oh, my God, just like he said—the old man.
Joan What old man?
Angela The gardener. It's just like he said. He said the police had been
   snoopin' around his shed. Dear God, the poor missus . . . (*She begins to
   cry*)
Commander (*coming round the bar to her; soothingly*) Don't cry, Angela.
   Look, you go off home. We'll be all right. The hotel's closed, and we
   can look after ourselves.

*Joan stands looking at them but her mind is miles away. She is thoughtful
and introverted, hardly noticing what is going on*

Angela (*wiping her eyes and blowing her nose heartily*) I think perhaps I
   will, sir. It's such a shock. I felt sure it was sleeping tablets, like she took
   before, and that's bad enough, God knows, but that poison. I know it's
   painful. My dad put it down for some rats once, he did, in our barn . . .
   oh, how they squealed, fair broke my 'eart 'earin' the poor things cryin'
   out like that . . . (*She begins to sob again*)
Commander (*putting his arm round her and leading her out*) Come on now,
   put on your coat, and I'll take you home.
Angela Oh, would you, sir, I'd be that grateful, I would . . . oh, you are
   kind . . .
Commander (*to Joan*) Won't be long. I'll just run her home.
Joan Yes, all right. I thought Rex would have been back by now, with
   Eva.
Commander I expect they stopped off for a noggin. You can't blame them.

He goes off with Angela

*Left alone Joan paces round restlessly, eventually coming to rest in the
armchair L.C. She sits, staring thoughtfully out front. There is the sound of a
car door slamming. She looks up expectantly*

   Rex enters looking haggard and fed up.

Rex Christ, I need a drink! (*He goes straight round behind the bar and
   pours himself a large Scotch*) Where's Roy off to? Making a getaway?
Joan He's taking Angela home. She's very upset—about the verdict.
Rex We're all upset! (*He drinks as if his life depended on it. Then he sighs
   with relief*) I needed that! What a morning! I don't think I've ever felt
   so bloody miserable. It was worse than the funeral. All those questions.
   I thought I was on trial.
Joan I think we all were—on trial.
Rex What do you mean?
Joan The police were here while we were away. They searched our rooms.
Rex God, what a bloody outrage!
Joan Roy said they were within their rights. They had a search warrant.
Rex But without asking anybody?
Joan I know, I was furious too.

Rex That calls for another drink. What about you?

Joan No thanks. Where's Eva? She came back with you, didn't she?

Rex She went upstairs to tidy up. She's not used to getting up so early. She said she felt a wreck.

Joan Ten o'clock is early for her.

There is a pause. Rex comes round the bar

Rex I suppose you'll be going back soon?

Joan I should go to-day. I only stayed for the inquest.

Rex (*quietly*) I shall miss you.

Joan Oh, I don't think so. You'll have Eva.

Rex That's just it.

Joan What do you mean? There's nothing now to stop you getting married. The hotel is all yours. Any—impediment to your future happiness has been removed.

Rex That's just it.

Joan What do you mean?

Rex (*sitting on the arm of the chair; speaking to her very seriously*) Listen, Joan, try to understand. I don't want to marry Eva. I never did. It was just—a bit of fun that's all.

Joan Like all the others.

Rex Yes, like all the others. I didn't intend her to take me seriously, I never do.

Joan Then tell her. I doubt whether *she*'ll commit suicide over it.

Rex (*moving away from her*) That was a nasty thing to say. I didn't know you had it in you, that sort of remark.

Joan There are lots of things you don't know about me.

Rex Apparently. (*He looks at her speculatively*) Oh, damn it all, Joan, I can't tell the girl. I want you to do it.

Joan (*with a short laugh*) My God, you haven't even got the guts to do your own dirty work. Celia was right about you: you are a very weak young man.

Rex Of course Celia was right. She's always been right. (*Turning away; his voice shaking with emotion*) And I miss her—terribly.

Joan (*surprised*) You do?

Rex (*with passion*) Of course I do. I need her. I didn't realize how much until now. I just don't know how I'm going to manage without her.

Joan (*after a pause, rising and moving up to the bar*) What a pity you didn't say so before.

Rex Before what?

Joan Before—she died, of course.

They stand looking at one another, Joan inscrutable and Rex puzzled when Eva enters through the archway. She is looking as pretty as ever and apparently not upset by the inquest, but she is furious

Eva Somebody has been in my room.

Joan I know.

Eva If it's that Angela I'll kill her. Going through my things, how dare she? You must give her the sack, Rex—

Joan (*quietly*) It wasn't Angela.

Eva Then who—

Joan The police were here while we were at the inquest.

Eva (*aghast*) Oh no! Then it was them!

Joan I'm afraid so.

Rex It's a damned cheek. I'm going to get on to the Chief Superintendent right away. (*He moves to the bar*)

Eva I should think so. The bloody gall of it.

Joan (*deliberately*) Did you have anything to hide?

Eva What are you getting at?

Joan Angela said they took something away from your room. A small bottle of pills for analysis.

Eva Oh God. (*She sinks down into the chair by the window*) I knew they were missing. I thought I'd just mislaid them at first.

Rex (*suspiciously*) What were they?

Eva Not cyanide if that's what you think.

Rex Of course I didn't imagine for a moment—

Eva Just some nice little pills that give me a nice little lift when I need it.

Joan (*with a sigh*) You told me you'd kicked that habit.

Eva (*evasively*) So I had. But when things get me down, like now, I've just gotta have something, some little extra help—drinking isn't the same, it isn't enough.

Rex Drugs, you mean?

Eva You're not shocked are you? Just harmless little things, really—

Rex Acid?

Eva No, I never got on to acid. Speed.

Rex (*thoughtfully*) I see. I should have guessed. All that refreshingly un-inhibited behaviour—it couldn't possibly have been natural.

Joan You're a fool, Eva.

Eva There's no harm in it.

Joan It's still against the law.

Eva (*frightened now*) What will they do to me?

Rex Lock you up, honey, for your own good.

Joan (*sharply*) Of course they won't. There'll be a fine, that's all.

Rex Doesn't that depend on whether it's a first offence?

There is a pause. Joan looks at Eva keenly

Joan There hasn't been another time, has there?

Eva (*with a shrug*) Oh, I was at a party once when we were having a few smokes, and the police raided it. Rotten pigs! They must have been tipped off!

Joan (*slowly*) Yes, I remember now. You told me about it. You got away with it though.

Eva I opened my big blue eyes and pleaded innocence! "Oh, Officer I didn't know what it was, cross my heart and hope to die!"

Rex And they believed you?

Eva They believed me. But still, they took my finger-prints and all that jazz.

Joan (*sighing wearily*) I just can't understand you. Why do you do such things?

Eva I enjoy it. The smoke's very pleasant. It makes you feel sexy.

Rex *You*'d hardly notice the difference.

Eva (*furiously*) What a rotten thing to say, you beast!

Joan Yes, Rex, I must object to that remark. It was most uncalled for.

Rex (*shrugs*) I apologize. Let's have another drink.

Eva (*stamping her foot; determined to have a row*) You don't care about me at all, really, do you? You're just like all the rest. In love with your own pleasure! Not me. It's nothing to do with me!

Rex Did I ever say anything about being in love with you?

Eva (*without her usual confidence*) I thought you did. I think you did.

Rex Then think harder. I'm always very careful not to mention the word. It doesn't figure in my vocabulary. (*He goes to the bar to pour himself another drink, and when he is there cannot resist adding with a sneer*) I certainly wouldn't use it to describe *our* relationship!

Eva You rotten pig! You want to offload me now because you think I'm trouble!

Rex Let's face it, I don't need you now!

Eva (*stung*) You don't need me! I suppose you needed old sour-puss then?

Rex (*with dangerous calm*) Who do you mean by that?

Eva You know exactly who I mean! Your damned, stupid, neurotic step-mother!

Rex (*glaring at her*) Be careful . . .

Joan Eva, be quiet. That's no way to talk with the woman just dead.

Eva (*recklessly*) Yes, dead, and I'm glad she's dead, do you hear?

Rex (*trying to control his temper*) Are you out of your tiny mind?

Eva No, I'm not. I know what I'm saying and I don't care! *She* wanted you all to herself, a vicious, jealous, possessive woman, that's what she was. Why did she do it? Why kill herself? Only to make us feel guilty, that's all! Well, I don't feel guilty, not a bit, why should I? Oh, the older generation are always getting at us, at the way we live. Look at them, they say, taking drugs, sleeping around, how disgusting! But at least we're natural. At least we don't fall in love with our relatives! Just because there's no other man around.

Rex (*going over to her menacingly*) What did you say?

Joan She didn't mean it! She doesn't know what's she's saying.

Eva Yes, I do. You can shut up. What do you know about anything, anyway? A man jilts you and you give up on life.

Joan (*horrified*) Stop it, Eva, please!

Eva You wouldn't begin to know what it is to be natural! You're like a woman wearing an iron girdle! It's your barrier against the world. Your barrier against getting hurt.

Joan (*pleading*) Eva, don't say any more!

Rex No, don't. (*He moves back to the bar*) I was going to hit you just now, but I really couldn't be bothered. You're just not worth it.

Eva You thought I was worth something in Brighton!

Rex I hadn't anything else to do at the time.

Eva (*trying to recover her pride*) It didn't matter to me. You don't really think it mattered, do you? Ask Joan, I'm always taking off with blokes. It's my way of life.

Rex I gathered that. (*On an impulse he reaches into the till and extracts a bundle of notes*) Here, I forgot to settle up! (*He throws them at her*)

Eva Oh, you beast! You swine! (*She flies at him, Joan goes after her to restrain her*) Let me get at him! I'll kill him!

Rex (*quite unperturbed*) I really think you would. Such passion! Do hold her tight, Joan, I should hate to have to knock her out.

Joan (*struggling with her*) Come on, Eva. Come and have a rest. You're overwrought. I've got some tranquillizers upstairs.

Eva (*calming down a bit*) Are you sure the police didn't take them, too?

Joan Don't be silly, dear. We'll sort it out between us. Don't worry about him. He really isn't worth it.

Eva *You* thought so.

Joan (*quickly*) No, no not really.

Eva Yes, you did, for years and years. Do you realize she's been carrying a torch around for you for years, ever since you first met? My God, I thought, this man must be something if my sister couldn't forget him after ten years. But you're not! You're not that good in any respect. I've had better!

Rex (*drily*) I'm sure you have, and many, many more!

Joan Don't be insulting, Rex. It isn't fair.

Rex Insulting? I thought she was proud of her promiscuity!

Eva Oh, let me get at him.

Joan No, no. Forget about him. We'll pack and go home. We don't have to stay here now.

Rex Yes, go on, go and leave a sinking ship.

Joan (*amused, despite herself*) That's not a very apt description of you, Rex. (*She begins to lead Eva away, her arm around her shoulders*)

Eva (*crying*) Nobody understands me, it isn't fair. Nobody cares, nobody understands. Everybody's against me . . .

Eva continues muttering as she and Joan go off with Joan soothing her.

Left alone Rex sighs unhappily, comes down-stage to the armchair and sits disconsolately

The Commander enters

Commander What's wrong with Eva? She's crying her eyes out.

Rex She fancies I insulted her.

Commander And did you?

Rex (*shrugging*) Who knows?

There is a pause. Roy wanders to the window and looks out

Commander It's all very strange, isn't it? Only a week ago Celia was still alive. We were talking together in this room. For the first time ever she was honest with me and told me all her troubles.

Rex Oh?

Commander I cared a great deal for her, you know, Rex. I suppose it's hard for you to understand because women are your hobby, but for me there's only ever been one woman.

Rex Shut up! (*He rises angrily*)

Commander What's wrong? What have I said?

Rex Don't talk about it—about her.

Commander All right, if that's the way you feel.

Rex It is. (*A pause*) I cared a lot for her too, more than you know, more than I knew myself. Now it's too late. (*He stops to steady his voice*) To think of her doing such a thing—because of me! And I've got to live with it for the rest of my life. (*He goes back to the bar abruptly and pours himself another drink*)

Commander What makes you—jump to that conclusion?

Rex What, that she did it because of me? She'd tried it before, you know.

Commander Ah yes, a *crie de coeur*, when she knew she would be stopped in time, that's not the same thing.

Rex We'd had a row that day. I was horrible to her. I couldn't repeat what I said. I just know I was horrible to her.

Commander (*with deliberate calm*) That is to assume that she committed suicide. That wasn't the verdict at the inquest, was it?

Rex No. But I thought they just needed more time. They have to establish her state of mind or something, don't they?

Commander They've had a week. That should be enough for them if they had no other suspicions.

Rex What—suspicions? You don't think it was an accident, do you?

Commander No, I don't think an intelligent person would take cyanide by accident.

Rex Well, then. (*He pauses, waiting for the Commander to speak, but as he says nothing he prompts him*) What do you think?

Commander I think it was murder.

There is a pause

Rex You can't be serious. Who would want to murder Celia?

Commander Who gains by her death?

Rex I do. (*Coming round the bar threateningly*) You're not seriously suggesting I would do such a thing? My God, if it weren't for your grey hairs . . .

Commander (*calmly*) I didn't accuse you. I simply said you gained by her death. If the police suspected you, you'd have been arrested by now.

Rex It's all in your own head. If they thought it was murder they'd have brought in a verdict of murder. That's the drill, isn't it? Murder by person or persons unknown.

Commander They're not sure, either way. Not yet.

Rex Then what makes you so suspicious? You know more than them, I suppose? Just because you were some sort of intelligence boffin in the war.

Commander I have a nose for a mystery, that's true. But if you used your common sense, you'd come to the same conclusion. The reason you haven't is because you've been suffering from shock all the week—yes, don't look surprised. I know you were cut up about her death. I don't think you're such a monster as all that.

Rex (*mollified*) Thank you. (*With sarcasm*) Have a drink?

Commander No, thanks.

Rex Well, go on, tell me more.

Commander It's a question of knowing the victim. In this case, Celia. I know she was highly strung and irrational at times, even a little unstable. I'm prepared to accept that she might have taken an overdose to scare you or threaten you, or some such reason. But I'm also sure that if she did that she'd make sure someone was within calling distance. I don't think she wanted to die. She had a strong will to live.

Rex Who hasn't?

Commander You haven't, for one. You'll be quite likely to destroy yourself slowly through drink, or just chasing pleasure.

Rex Thanks a lot!

Commander But Celia wasn't like that. She was full of life, vibrant, with a strong will to live.

Rex But she still took an overdose, previously.

Commander (*patiently*) Yes, she did, but not to die, only to threaten. If she'd have wanted to do that this time she would certainly not have taken cyanide.

Rex Why not?

Commander Because it's swift, painful and irreversible. Nazi war criminals took that way out when there was no other. But, nobody would make such a conscious choice, not when they can simply take a sweet overdose and go out on a cloud of euphoria. (*Pause*) Did you see her face?

Rex (*shudders*) Yes. (*He takes a swift drink*) It was awful!

Commander Well, then. It wasn't suicide. I'm convinced of it.

Rex (*in awe*) But murder, Roy, that's hard to accept. Who would do such a thing?

They stand looking at one another. There is a pause. Then a slight tap on the french windows. George Carter is there

George 'Ere open up!

Commander (*going over and opening the french windows*) What is it?

George There's a police car coming up the drive. I thought you'd like to know.

Commander O.K. I'll see to it. (*He is about to shut the window when George stops him*)

George What 'appened, sir?

Commander When?

George At the inquest like. I mean I'm bound to be interested, on account of it was my poison, wasn't it, that the missus took? My poison what was in my shed. I told 'em all in the village pub last night, I did.

Commander (*drily*) You must be very proud of it.

George Oh, I wouldn't say that. Still, I am an interested party, aren't I? I've got a right to know.
Commander (*shortly*) The inquest was adjourned.
George Oh, why?
Rex Because they don't know, they're not sure how or why my step-mother died, that's why.
George I see. Well, that's not much to tell 'em down at the pub. They'll be disappointed like.
Rex (*with heavy sarcasm*) Oh, I *am* sorry.
Commander I'll go and see what the police want, shall I?
Rex Yes, please. I'm beginning to feel a bit under the weather.
Commander I thought you might be.

He goes towards the archway as Joan enters

Joan (*nervously*) The police are here again. That Inspector.
Commander I'll deal with them.

He goes out to R. *of archway*

George stands outside the french window, too curious to go away. Joan goes over to Rex, who is behind the bar

Joan (*unhappily*) I suppose it's about Eva. Oh dear, what am I to do, Rex?
Rex I dunno, don't ask me. I'm the hopeless, unreliable, useless young man, remember?
Joan I've never said that.
Rex You've implied it. Lost without a strong woman, that's me. Let's have another drink. (*He helps himself to another drink. By now he is quite drunk*)
Joan (*anxiously*) Do you think you should? Haven't you had enough?
Rex (*angrily*) Don't nag, woman! Nobody nags Rex, not any more. Do you hear.
Joan Yes, I hear. Does it help—to get drunk?
Rex It helps. Do you want one? (*He comes round the bar*)
Joan No thank you. (*After a pause, looking at him thoughtfully*) I'm sorry about that scene just now—with Eva.
Rex That's all right. Forget it. We all say things we don't mean sometimes. I was unkind myself. I'm upset you see, today. (*He sways on his feet. He is feeling very sorry for himself*)
Joan (*sympathetically*) I understand.
Rex Do you, little Miss School-teacher? I doubt whether you do. I doubt whether anyone understands. Celia was the one who understood. She always did. I can't believe she's gone. (*Becoming maudlin*) I can remember when she first came here. She was pretty, and the old boy tried something right away. But she soon slapped him down. He admired her for it, too. He told me. He always told me about his women. "Blast her, if she didn't shut me out, boy, locked her door on me, in me own hotel." He couldn't get over it. They'd always given in sooner or later. He knew how to spoil them, you see, and he had charm. He'd buy them things,

jewellery, pretty clothes, he always won them round in the end, but not Celia. She wasn't that kind of a girl.

Joan Funny, that someone like you should respect virtue!

Rex Why, someone like me? It's rakes like me who do respect it, because we don't see much of it. Celia had all the opportunities going. There were always men here ready to bed her down, but she wouldn't have it. Not her!

Joan (*crisply*) She was clever!

Rex What?

Joan She held out for high stakes, that was clever!

Rex I won't hear a word against her.

Joan Of course not. I wouldn't dream of saying anything against her. I admired her. She knew what she wanted and she went after it. That takes courage. It takes both courage and strength to hurt people.

Rex (*confused*) She didn't hurt people. Not her. It was me. I was the one. I was always hurting people.

Joan You don't mean to. You're just thoughtless. I understand.

Rex Do you? (*He looks at her thoughtfully*) What was it Eva said just now about you being jilted?

Joan (*evasively*) Oh, nothing. Just something that happened last year. It doesn't matter now.

Rex Won't you tell me?

Joan (*reluctantly*) I was going to get married last year. He was a teacher, too. But . . . (*She shrugs unhappily, unable to find the right words*)

Rex Eva spoilt it for you?

Joan (*evasively*) You could say that.

Rex I think I can guess how.

Before Joan can answer the Commander comes in through the archway looking worried

Commander Joan, could I have a word with you for a moment?

Joan Of course, what about? (*Guessing by his grave expression*) It's the police, isn't it? They want Eva.

Commander Yes, they want to take her to the station for questioning.

Joan (*miserably*) All right, I'll tell her. I do think they might have made allowances though, today of all days. (*She goes to pass him, and he stops her*)

Commander I haven't told you why.

Joan It's about the drugs, isn't it? The pills they found in her bedroom.

Commander No, it isn't about that.

Joan (*puzzled*) Then what?

Commander (*slowly and deliberately*) They want to question her in connection with the murder of Celia Randolph. (*There is a slight pause while Joan takes a step back, aghast*) I'm sorry.

There is another pause while the fact sinks in with all of them. They have forgotten that George is still standing in the french window opening. When he speaks they all turn to look at him

George (*triumphantly*) I could've told you that.

Commander What do you mean?

George (*chuckling*) I knew all along. Nobody bothered to ask me till today. I could've told 'em before if they'd bothered. They didn't think I knew nothing.

Rex What are you getting at, you old ruin?

George I knowed it was her, 'cos I saw her. (*He pauses for effect, pleased with himself*) I saw her that night, down there in my shed. I saw her takin' the stuff. So you see, I knowed all along it was her!

He smiles round at them, delighted, as—

the CURTAIN *falls*

SCENE 2

The same. Early next morning

There is a dishevelled look about the room. Rex is hunched in the armchair looking tired and miserable. His feet are up on a stool, his tie undone, an empty whisky bottle by the side of the chair and a glass on the table. The Commander enters with newspapers under his arm. He looks surprised at seeing Rex

Commander You're up early.

Rex (*disconsolately*) I haven't been to bed. I couldn't sleep. I watched the dawn come up. First time I've done that since I was a Boy Scout.

Commander No, I didn't sleep very well, either. (*Nevertheless he seems to be in much better spirits than Rex and looks refreshed*) The walk did me good. Down to the village and back.

Rex Your usual constitutional. Get the papers?

Commander Yes. (*He puts them down on the small table by the armchair*) There's nothing like an early morning walk to clear the head.

Rex I agree there's nothing like an early morning walk—nothing so bloody awful! I hate being up this early. I don't feel quite human. I suppose I ought to have a shave. (*He rubs his chin ruminatively*) We haven't a sweet young thing in the kitchen to wait on us so perhaps I'd better make some tea as well. I think I can just about manage that.

Commander Before you go I want to have a word with you.

Rex (*resigned, but weary*) All right, but I know what it's about and I must say I'm sick of the subject.

Commander I know. I do understand how you feel. (*He is curiously excited*) Only I've been working things out this morning. It's quite— fascinating . . .

Rex You're in a funny mood. You seem to have forgotten all about Celia.

Commander No, I haven't, not at all. But I'm determined justice shall be done.

Rex It will be, won't it?

Commander You're quite convinced Eva did it?

Rex Yes, aren't you?

Commander Tell me your reasons.

Rex Must I? (*He sighs wearily*) I've been over and over it in my head all night. I wonder if you know what it's like to be tortured with remorse.

Commander Why are you so remorseful all of a sudden?

Rex There's nothing sudden about it. Of course I'm remorseful. It was all my fault, wasn't it? I've gone over it again and again, all night long. What did I say and when did I say it? When did I put the idea into her head to murder Celia? It must have been my fault. She wouldn't have done it otherwise. But I swear I didn't mean it. (*Pathetically, imploring the Commander to understand*) Do you believe me?

Commander Yes, I believe you. You're as much a victim of your own charm as the women are. I really don't think you can help it. Women like you. It's difficult for you not to take advantage of that fact.

Rex (*relieved*) Well, thanks.

Commander I don't blame you for that. I don't blame you for philandering. I do blame you for lying, but given your character and your circumstances I might well have behaved in the same way.

Rex (*frowning*) I'm not so sure I like that.

Commander Anyway, there's no point in going over all that any more. Celia is dead and I miss her terribly. But I'm going to make quite sure her murderer doesn't profit by her death.

Rex She won't if she's imprisoned for yonks!

Commander Then we've got to make sure the case sticks.

Rex (*fatigued*) Can't we leave all that to the police?

Commander I don't think we can. It's all very flimsy. Besides, she might easily say you put her up to it, and then where will we be?

Rex You don't think she'd do that?

Commander Why not? You were the one to benefit, after all. She might rather plead guilty to accessory than to murder—and get a lighter sentence!

Rex (*perturbed*) My God, the little bitch! You don't think she would?

Commander She might! That's why you've got to help me.

Rex Yes, of course. (*He is immediately more alert. They put their heads together, seated one either side of the table down-stage R.*) What do you want to know?

Commander Let's think about that day last week when you came back from Brighton.

Rex When—it happened, you mean?

Commander Yes. What time was it when you came home?

Rex I'm not sure. It was after dinner, because we'd missed it and we were both hungry.

Commander Before nine? It must have been, because I was in here talking to Celia.

Rex Yes, it was definitely before nine.

Commander Tell me all your movements from the minute you came in.

Rex I can't remember. I was a bit smashed.

Commander Try.

Rex We came in. You were here. We talked, had another drink. You went out, I think.

Commander That's right.

Rex Then Eva went upstairs to change, or rest, or something, then I had a little chat with Celia, more of a short, sharp exchange of words, really, and then, I don't know, well, we were all here, weren't we? Later on.

Commander Eva definitely left you for a while?

Rex Yes.

Commander So that was when the old man saw her down in the shed, it must have been, just about nine, as he said. (*He pauses deep in thought*)

Rex Exactly, he saw her, that's surely conclusive? How do you think she managed the rest of it?

Commander Quite easily, really.

Rex It was in the sleeping-pills, wasn't it? The stuff.

Commander Yes, there's no doubt about that. Celia always kept them by her bedside, and they were capsules, conveniently for the murderer, not pills or tablets. That might have presented a problem.

Rex Why?

Commander Because it's quite a simple matter to take those gelatine capsules apart and fill them with some other substance, particularly if, like Eva, you're used to messing about with drugs.

Rex (*slowly*) So that's what she did. The police must know that, of course, they took the rest of the bottle away with them.

Commander Yes, they haven't told us but I daresay several of them were doctored up in that way, just to make sure. It didn't matter when Celia took the poison as long as she took it eventually. I daresay the murderer would have preferred it to be when she was miles away from here, however. It was bad luck it happened that self-same night.

Rex I suppose so. (*As a thought occurs to him*) But Eva had no plans to leave here. On the contrary—

Commander Yes, I've thought of that. (*There is a pause, then Roy adds abruptly*) When you were in Brighton did Eva wear her wig?

Rex No, she couldn't find it. Why?

Commander Just an idea I've got.

Rex But you're not going to tell me.

Commander Yes, I will tell you, but later on. (*With deliberation*) I'm still not completely sure you're not implicated.

Rex For God's sake, Roy . . . (*He rises angrily and moves down-stage* R.)

Joan enters. She looks serene and is wearing something brighter and prettier than usual. She is carrying a tray with tea things

Joan I've made some tea.

Commander Oh, good! Just what we need!

Joan (*she puts the tray on the table down-stage* R.) I thought I'd better since we haven't any staff.

Commander (*agreeably*) That is good of you, isn't it, Rex?

Rex (*returning to his disgruntled state*) Yes, very. I think I'll go and shave first if you don't mind. I feel a wreck.

Joan Oh, all right, but don't be long. Tea's horrible if it's stewed.
Rex All right.

He gives Roy a perplexed look and exits through the archway

Joan (*sitting and pouring out the tea*) I'll make you some toast if you like.
Commander No, this is fine. I never take breakfast.
Joan When do you think Angela will be back?
Commander Oh, soon, I expect, when she's got over the shock of it all.
(*He sits to drink his tea*) It's nice of you to be so concerned.
Joan Of course I'm concerned.
Commander Aren't you going back? Your term must have started by
now.
Joan (*quite serenely*) Yes, it has. I rang the Head up last night and told her
I wasn't going back at all.
Commander (*sharply*) Why is that?
Joan Surely it's obvious? I shall have to stay here and help Eva in her
defence. The Head was furious of course, but I expect she'll understand
when the facts sink in. After all, it isn't every day one's young sister is
accused of murder.
Commander She hasn't actually been accused yet, has she?
Joan No, but they'll have to charge her, won't they? They can't keep her
indefinitely without charging her. I thought I'd go into Lewes today and
try to see her. Do you think they'll let me?
Commander I don't know.
Joan I want to get her the best possible lawyer. I have some money put
by, I don't care what it costs. I'll sell the house if necessary.
Commander (*thoughtfully*) You seem awfully sure she did it.
Joan (*surprised*) Of course, I am. Aren't you?
Commander I suppose I must be.
Joan After all, she had motive and opportunity. Those are the two
important ingredients, aren't they? She said in front of all of us that she
wanted to get rid of Rex's step-mother.
Commander Yes, I know she did, but people often say things they don't
really mean, particularly when they're drunk or on drugs, or both.
Besides, getting rid of her didn't necessarily mean murder.
Joan No, it didn't. But then, there's the other thing, the fact that the
gardener saw her in the shed. Why should she go down there if not to
get the poison?
Commander That's true. (*He pauses*) I must say you're taking it all very
calmly.
Joan Yes I am. (*patiently*) I can see you think it's odd, but Eva has been a
great worry to me for a long time. I've always been afraid something
really disastrous would happen. Now it has happened, it's almost a
relief. Surely you understand that?
Commander Yes, I do. It's like in the war when you can hear the bombs
falling all around you. It was a relief when they exploded over somebody else. It was the one you didn't hear that hit you!
Joan That isn't quite what I meant.

Commander I must say, though, I didn't expect you to be quite so—relaxed. Almost happy.

Joan (*quickly*) Oh no, I'm not happy. How can I be with my sister in gaol for murder? Oh, no, I'm certainly not happy, but I'm not exactly unhappy either. It will be a challenge, helping her and helping Rex. I always function better when I'm up against it.

Commander You intend to help Rex as well. How altruistic!

Joan Not at all! I—I feel responsible in a way—for all this trouble.

Commander How?

Joan (*hesitantly*) Well, Eva is my responsibility. I should have realized a long time ago that she needed treatment for her drug-taking and so on. I just didn't accept she was any sort of danger, except to herself.

Commander You can't blame yourself.

Joan But I do. I've been over-protective to her. If only I'd let her face up to life on her own, just once, but I never did! I complained about having to help her out of various scrapes but I went on doing it.

Commander Love can be a great burden.

Joan Love?

Commander Your love for your sister.

Joan (*irritably*) It was more duty than love. I think I ceased to love her, once she grew up. She was a sweet little girl. I suppose you find that hard to believe?

Commander Not at all. I find it easy to believe. I would say you ceased to love her when she broke your engagement for you.

Joan (*surprised*) What?

Commander You didn't realize I knew about that?

Joan No, I didn't. (*Chagrined*) I thought Rex could be trusted with a confidence.

Commander Rex didn't tell me. It was Eva herself. That very first evening. I helped her up the stairs, if you remember. She was well gone. "My sister hates me", she said, with the truthful tongue of the very drunk, "because I stole her fiancé from her."

Joan (*crisply*) That's absurd.

Commander Is it? There's not a grain of truth in it?

Joan (*evasively*) I wouldn't say that. I was engaged last year, it's true.

Commander And what happened?

Joan We found we weren't suited after all. We broke it off. It was a mutual arrangement.

Commander You weren't hurt?

Joan Of course not. (*She avoids the Commander's eyes, adding, with sudden fury*) You can't believe a thing Eva says. Everybody knows she's a liar.

Commander (*thoughtfully*) It had the ring of truth. It just occurred to me that it might have been the very thing that turned you.

Joan Turned me? What do you mean?

Commander Made you bitter and twisted, that was the old phrase, wasn't it? There was this young sister you'd done so much for, made sacrifices, no doubt of your own happiness, and then she comes between you, you and the man you intend to marry. It could upset some people deeply, if they were not quite well-balanced.

Joan (*stiffly*) Of course I'm well-balanced. I object to your insinuations.

Commander And then I thought to myself, perhaps you started to think about the past, about the time in your youth when you had been happy, in love for the first time. It's always a romantic period for a girl, and the memories over the years would have softened and mellowed and taken on a very seductive, golden quality. I can understand it. There was this beautiful old place, and long, hot summer days. You were on the threshold of a new career and full of hope and sparkle. Then there was Rex, as debonair, no doubt, in your eyes as Errol Flynn. Just because you were intelligent it didn't mean you had no romantic, girlish fancies. You still have. Only you stifle them now. Yes, I realized right away just how much that holiday romance meant to you.

Joan (*recovering her composure*) I don't deny it meant something once.

Commander But not any more?

Joan Of course not. (*With irritation*) I'm beginning to find this conversation rather tiresome.

Commander And I'm beginning to find it rather interesting. Stimulating, almost. I'd forgotten how much I missed my work.

Joan I can't see that this situation is remotely similar.

Commander Oh, but it is. Pitting one's wits against another. It's like a game of chess, and I think I have you in check-mate.

Joan I think not.

Commander The police might be prepared to accept that your sister was infatuated enough with Rex to kill for him, but I do not.

Joan It doesn't really matter what you think.

Commander On the other hand, somebody like yourself in love with that same young man—

Joan I keep telling you I'm not.

Commander But you were.

Joan Yes, once, a long time ago, not any more!

Commander Then why did you come back, after all these years?

Joan (*with a shrug*) Curiosity.

Commander Is that all? Not a need to wallow in nostalgia? To escape into the past where once you had been happy, happy and you thought loved?

Joan (*becoming exasperated*) No, not at all!

Commander (*hounding her*) But it wasn't what you expected, was it? Oh, Rex was still here, the same as ever, still unattached, immature and irresponsible. Just the sort of man you need to make you feel useful, someone to look after, someone to mother, someone to dominate.

Joan I'd had enough of that with Eva. That isn't what I want in a man at all.

Commander You deceive yourself, Joan. That's just what you want. His weakness adds to your strength. A strong man would frighten you to death.

Joan (*tensely*) You don't know what you're talking about.

Commander (*ignoring this*) At first those ten years must have fallen away as if they'd never been. Rex was still here, and you still wanted him. But he wasn't as free as he appeared, was he? There was Celia.

Joan (*catching at this*) Yes, there was Celia. She made quite sure she tied him down, making him financially dependent on her, smothering his initiative.

Commander (*almost laughing*) You can't believe that! Rex was a very willing prisoner. He likes an easy life. He wasn't struggling to be free. What a shock for you. So almost yours, wasn't he? (*Taunting her*) How unbearable to lose him twice. Particularly for you, Joan. You're not a good loser, are you?

Joan (*with apparent boredom*) How long must I submit to this character analysis? Is there a charge?

Commander Sneer if you like. You know I'm approaching the truth, and it worries you.

Joan I assure you I'm not in the least worried. Perhaps you should inspect your own conscience.

Commander What do you mean by that? My conscience is clear.

Joan (*pleased as she tries to turn the tables on him*) Is it? Perhaps all this fuss is to obscure another issue, a deeper one. You're afraid that the police might unearth some unpleasant facts about Mr Randolph's death.

Commander (*surprised*) What? What are you talking about? The old man had a heart attack.

Joan How do we know that? There wasn't an inquest. He died very conveniently for Celia, didn't he? Leaving her the hotel, cutting Rex out of his will. He might have changed his mind again if he'd lived a bit longer.

Commander (*shrewdly*) Attack is the best method of defence, that's it, is it?

Joan It's a possibility, isn't it? It's worth investigating. Perhaps Celia took the cyanide by accident. Perhaps those pills were left over from last year when she poisoned her husband.

Commander (*with a ghost of a smile*) A good try, but it won't work. Even a country doctor can tell the difference between cyanide poisoning and a heart attack. Besides, the old boy wasn't cremated. The body can always be exhumed. So I shouldn't pursue that tactic if I were you.

Joan There was a lot of talk in the village.

Commander Village gossip! Of course there was talk. Celia was the sort of person who inspired talk, so many people were jealous of her, including yourself!

Joan (*crisply*) Nonsense!

Commander Anyway, where does Eva fit into this theory of yours? If Celia's death was accidental it lets Eva off the hook. That's not what you want, is it?

Joan Of course it is—my own sister! Of course I want her to be released.

Commander Oh no, Joan, that's not part of your plan. You've eliminated one rival. You still have the other one to deal with.

There is a pause. Joan turns away from him and picks up the tray, but her hands are trembling and she has to put it down again

Rex enters

Rex (*cheerfully*) I feel better now. I could face tea and toast.
Joan (*tonelessly*) I'll have to make some more. (*But she doesn't move*)
Rex (*looking from one to the other of them*) Is anything wrong?
Commander No, not at all.
Joan (*still not moving*) I'll make some more.
Rex Are you all right? (*He looks at the Commander and taps his head*) The strain, old boy?
Joan (*impulsively*) Rex, you must try to understand something!
Rex What? I'm up to here with trying to understand.
Joan (*urgently*) About Eva. I don't want you to hate her. Whatever she did, she did for you, to set you free.
Rex I *am* free. What do you mean?
Joan It was a grand gesture. Don't you see? In its own way, magnificent, like Hedda Gabbler, dying beautifully! Ibsen understood what it was to make a grand gesture, to leave an indelible footprint on the sands of time. So that people know you have been there.
Commander (*severely*) That's a poor justification for murder.
Joan Murder or suicide, what's the difference? It's the gesture that counts. We all have to die sooner or later. Most of us just drift towards death like sheep or cattle, never taking any positive action, without a will of our own. How magnificent, just once, to take a hand! To stand up against Fate and refuse to accept the way things are. To make something happen.
Rex (*puzzled*) Roy, what is she on about?
Commander (*quickly, not wanting her to stop*) Go on, Joan, let's hear some more of your unique philosophy.
Joan (*pleased, warming to the subject*) We're all full of destructive tendencies. You can't deny it. Women are no less violent than men, you should just hear them talking about one another, even in little girls it's there, hatred in their voices. But we have to hide it, we have to hide our hatred because it isn't polite, it's too shocking. So we smile and smother our anger and go on being courteous to one another. (*She is tense with repressed anger. She manages to go on after a pause*) We're supposed to be civilized. We don't give way to murderous impulses like savages. But just once, imagine, how splendid to break free! To indulge in a violent act, against society, against the law—above it, yes, above it . . . (*She has forgotten them. She comes back to reality with an effort, afraid that she has said too much, trying to justify herself*) Eva, Eva indulged a murderous impulse. But it doesn't make her bad. Don't you see? In a way, it makes her better than us, more free. Just once she did something of her own volition, something no-one could ever change.
Commander But Eva was always doing things of her own volition. It wouldn't make her more free to indulge one more selfish whim, would it?

He begins to edge to within sight of the window

Joan It would. It did. Don't you see? I want Rex to understand, so that he doesn't hate her. (*Going to him*)

Rex I don't hate her.

Joan You don't?

Commander (*quickly and calmly*) Like me, Rex is not convinced that Eva did it. Nor apparently are the police. (*Looking towards the window*) Look, Rex, do you see anything?

Rex (*going to the window*) Good lord, it looks like Eva. Look, Joan, over there by the shed.

Joan What, Eva? No, no, it can't be. (*She goes over to the window*)

Rex She's moving away, towards the house. She'll be coming in. (*Going back to the Commander*) What a turn-up for the books! They couldn't hold her then. Not enough evidence, I expect that's it. Perhaps they've decided it was suicide after all.

Joan (*to the Commander*) Was it Eva? I couldn't see very well from here. Just the sunlight on her hair, a flash of bright colour . . .

Commander That's right, wearing her wig.

Joan gives him a sharp look, and bites her lips. There is a tap at the window

George enters excitedly

George I see her. I see her again, clear as clear, walking towards the 'ouse. They've let her out then. Didn't they believe me, or what?

Commander They believed you. So did I. You told us the truth as you saw it, but was the truth what you saw?

Rex I wish I knew what was going on.

Commander You will. Come in now, Angela.

Angela appears in the archway from the R. wearing Eva's blonde wig

Rex What is this masquerade? Why have you got the girl done up like that?

Commander Old George thought he saw Eva just now in the garden, but he saw Angela. The reason is that George had only ever seen Eva as a blonde. Any girl, reasonably similar in build, could have been mistaken for her in the dark of the shed, and in the gloom of a September evening. That's what Joan relied on. She wanted to be seen out there, but she wanted to be seen as Eva, not as herself. George nearly spoiled the plan by keeping the information to himself to create more interest. It must have been quite a worry for you. (*He addresses Joan*)

Joan (*guardedly*) I don't know what you mean. It's all ridiculous!

Commander Is it? We'll see. (*He goes towards the exit*) Perhaps you'd better phone for the police, Angela. (*turning to Joan*) I take it you're not going anywhere?

He goes off with Angela to the R. of the archway

Angela (*as they go; to the Commander*) I was all right, was I? That's what you wanted me to do?

Commander Yes, yes, you were excellent. Ever thought of going on the stage?

Joan stands by herself, down-stage L. *Rex looks at her thoughtfully, then he turns to George*

Rex All right, George, thanks for everything. I'll call you if I want you.

George (*taking the hint*) I'm goin'. I'm goin'. I'm sorry I made a mistake like that, but I'm not 'avin' people say it's my eyesight. My eyes are as good as most people's and better'n some. But it's like the Commander said, at that time of night, and from a distance, it's easy to make a mistake. 'Ow was I to know she wore a wig? God bless us . . .

Rex (*impatiently*) Yes, we'll sort it out. Don't worry! It doesn't matter now. (*He closes the windows firmly in George's face*)

George stands resentfully for a moment and then, still muttering to himself, goes off

Rex turns round slowly to look at Joan

You did it? You really did it? (*He sounds as if he is not quite convinced*)

Joan (*seizing the opportunity to exonerate herself*) No, of course not. You don't believe him, do you? He's just trying to be clever. He has to justify his existence. He can't prove a thing.

Rex I wonder. (*He gives her a shrewd look*)

Joan Of course he can't. The old boy doesn't know who he saw. He's not much of a witness. It could even have been Angela.

Rex No, it couldn't have been Angela. We passed her on our way through the village riding pillion on her boyfriend's motor bike. No, it certainly wasn't Angela.

Joan Then it was Eva. She had time. You were in here drinking. You couldn't swear to how long she was out of your company. She did it then.

Rex (*thoughtfully*) I wonder. Is it really possible?

Joan Of course it's possible.

Rex I don't mean the mechanics of the thing. I mean is Eva really capable of murder? That's the thing that has rankled with me all the time. It's so hard to believe that she would do anything quite so—desperate. And all for me. (*He goes up to the bar. There is a pause. Joan looks at him guardedly*) All for me. (*He pours himself a drink*) Terrible, isn't it? But flattering too, in a way. I didn't know I could inspire such passion. Do you want one? (*He indicates the bottle*)

Joan No, no, I mustn't fuddle my brain. I must be free to think.

Rex Yes, you must. (*He comes round the bar to her*) You have an ordeal in front of you but you'll come out of it all right. Roy's theory is, after all, only a theory. No concrete proof.

Joan No, exactly, no proof at all.

Rex So dear little Eva killed for me. Well!

Joan (*puzzled*) You sound as if you admire her.

Rex Naturally, I do. I didn't realize she had it in her. Of course, I don't approve, but at the same time I can't resist a sneaking admiration. As you said yourself it was a grand gesture. And it was all for me. (*He sounds complacent*) She'll go to prison, of course, for a long time, but when she comes out I'll be waiting. It's the least I can do. She'll still be

young. She has youth on her side. I'll keep the hotel going somehow and
we'll make some sort of life together—afterwards. Why not? I owe it to
her, in a way.

Joan (*with a strangled cry*) No!

Rex What?

Joan No, that's not what I want. That's not the way I want it to be.

Rex Why not? I thought you'd be pleased. At least I shall stand by your
sister.

Joan No, no, no. She doesn't deserve you. She's always had everything.
She doesn't deserve you as well.

Rex I thought the general consensus of opinion was that we deserved one
another!

Joan You don't really believe Eva could kill for love, do you? She hasn't
got it in her. She hasn't any real emotions, just silly, spurious little
feelings: lust, envy, greed, she can feel things like that, but not love, not
love that eats into your soul, that takes over your mind, that robs you of
sleep night after night. What does such a girl know of love? She's a
surface person, nothing deep has ever touched her. She couldn't risk
everything for love. She doesn't care enough. How could you believe it
of her? She hasn't got the guts!

Rex (*slowly*) No, you're right, she hasn't, but *you* have.

Joan Yes, I have.

Rex (*in quiet triumph*) As I thought!

Joan (*realizing that she has betrayed herself but no longer trying to hide her
guilt*) But I did it for you!

Rex (*scornfully*) For me?

Joan Yes, yes, so that you could be free, so that you could have your own
birthright, so that you could, we could . . . (*She hesitates before his
obvious contempt*)

Rex So that we could what? You don't really think I'd look at you, free
or not, do you?

Joan I thought you might. You did once.

Rex Did I? (*With slow deliberation*) I'll tell you something, and I hope it
hurts. I couldn't even remember you! That great love affair of your life
meant nothing to me, do you hear?

Joan (*disbelievingly*) You don't mean that!

Rex Of course I do. Take a look at yourself. You're not even my type!

Joan But I am, I am. I'm strong and dependable, just like Celia. She knew
you needed a strong woman to lean on—

Rex (*furiously*) Shut up!

Joan (*startled*) What?

Rex You don't really think you could take her place, do you? Do you?

Joan I don't know. I thought I could.

Rex You stupid little bitch! Nobody could ever take her place, ever, do
you hear? She meant ten times more to me than any of the stupid little
birds I've played around with. I needed her. I really needed her. (*His
voice breaks and he turns away*) The trouble is I didn't realize it until it
was too late.

Joan (*after a pause, miserably*) I didn't know. If only I'd known!

The Commander returns with Angela, who is holding the wig in her hand

Commander The police are on their way. You'd better get ready.

Joan (*with an effort controlling herself and with a certain dignity now*) Of course!

Commander I'll come with you, while you pack.

Joan (*stopping in the archway by Angela and taking the wig out of her hand*) If only I'd burned the bloody thing!

She tosses it over her shoulder and goes off. The Commander gives Rex a last look of triumph and follows her

Angela looks across at Rex unhappily and then runs over to him and begins to cry on his shoulder. Rex soothes her gently, a cynical smile on his face as—

the CURTAIN *falls*

FURNITURE AND PROPERTY LIST

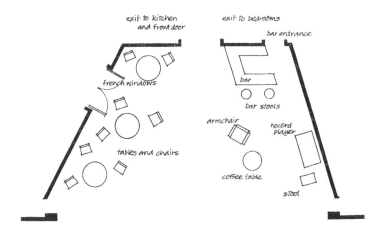

exit to kitchen and front door

exit to bedrooms

bar entrance

french windows

bar

bar stools

armchair

record player

tables and chairs

coffee table

stool

ACT I

SCENE 1

On stage: Bar. *On it:* jug of water, soda water, ashtray, bar mats, till. *Behind it:* bottles on optics, display of various bottles of spitits, including whisky and gin, minerals, glasses, etc.
3 tables
1 coffee table
Several chairs
1 armchair
Bar stools
Small stool
Record-player
Carpet
Window curtains
Dressing at the discretion of the producer

Off stage: Tray, marmalade in dish, toast on rack, teapot, milk, sugar (**Angela**)
Newspapers (**Commander**)
Shears (**George**)
Small bottle of vinegar, cotton wool (**Celia**)

Personal: **Eva:** cigarettes, lighter
Rex: £1 note

SCENE 2

Strike:	Table cloth from table, dirty glasses
Set:	Coffee cup on downstage table "78" records on floor and table
Off stage:	Tray (**Angela**)
Personal:	**Commander:** money **Celia:** bottle of capsules

ACT II

SCENE 1

Strike:	Records, bottle of capsules
Set:	Dirty glasses on bar and table Bundle of pound notes in till
Personal:	**Angela:** duster, handkerchief

SCENE 2

Set:	Whisky bottle and glasses on table downstage L.
Off stage:	Tray with three cups and saucers, tea in pot, milk, sugar (**Joan**)
Personal:	**Commander:** newspapers **Angela:** wig

LIGHTING PLOT

Property fittings required: wall lights
Interior. A bar/lounge. The same throughout

ACT I, SCENE 1
To open: general morning light
No cues

ACT I, SCENE 2
To open: wall lights on
No cues

ACT II, SCENE 1
To open: midday sunlight
No cues

ACT II, SCENE 2
To open: early morning light
No cues

EFFECTS PLOT

ACT I

SCENE 1

No cues

SCENE 2

ACT II

SCENE 1

SCENE 2

No cues

MADE AND PRINTED IN GREAT BRITAIN BY
LATIMER TREND & COMPANY LTD PLYMOUTH

MADE IN ENGLAND

Lightning Source UK Ltd.
Milton Keynes UK
UKOW06f0224230515

252112UK00001B/6/P